Pave Your Own Way

13 Skills to Create Your Professional Success

CAROLINA APONTE

All my Best,
CAROLINA

SPARK Publications
Charlotte, North Carolina

Pave Your Own Way:
13 Skills to Create Your Professional Success
Carolina Aponte

Designed, produced, and published by SPARK Publications
SPARKpublications.com
Charlotte, North Carolina

Paperback, October 2020, ISBN: 978-1-943070-96-1
Library of Congress Control Number: 2020914752

For my daughters
Gabriella and Adriana,
may your own paths
lead you to much
happiness and success!

For Jasmine,
I am proud of the road you are paving.
Continue making a difference in the world.

To everyone I have met,
I am thankful our paths have crossed.

Contents

Preface

As I started a new chapter in my personal life, I began to open my mind and my heart to the messages I kept receiving from friends, business associates, and even strangers: share my story with the world by writing a book documenting my personal journey as an immigrant to the United States (especially to counter the current narrative about immigrants in this country), and the many lessons that led me to live a life they admire. Repeatedly, I heard that the energy and enthusiasm I emanate is something people are attracted to and seek out. I received affirmations even when I wasn't searching for them, and soon it became clear that I would write a book to share how I turned the obstacles I encountered into a mindset of determination, perseverance, and positivity.

In this book, I share wisdom and practical activities with those who are either at a loss of where to even begin, or those who are ready to take their own destinies by the horns and make their dreams come true.

So here we are, as with all things that matter, at the very beginning of my story and how I developed the mindsets and skills needed to achieve the life I now enjoy. I was born in Caracas, Venezuela, in the spring of 1967, a year that brought many changes to my family. My parents, Jose and Julieta, already had three kids, ages twelve, eleven, and nine, when they found out they were going to have a fourth child, me. They lived in a small apartment in the city, and my dad traveled the country as a paint salesman.

The night of July 29, 1967, my dad was away on business, and my mom, my siblings, and I were in the apartment. My mom was watching TV, and my siblings were playing, when a 6.5 magnitude earthquake shook Caracas, causing severe damage to the city. When the tremors stopped, my mom carried me down the stairs with my sister and brothers running alongside and piled us into our family car to be safe from harm.

The earthquake and one brother's ongoing asthma pushed my parents to decide to move away from the city to Isla de Margarita—a small island in the Caribbean with more than fifty beaches and the best empanadas I've ever tasted. The island's status as a duty-free port just twenty miles from the mainland, and fifty minutes by frequent flights from Caracas, made it a mecca for local tourism and business opportunities.

My parents packed and moved us to the island and began their own entrepreneurial journey by starting several small businesses, failing, and eventually building a successful business that supported the family for many years. Eventually, the country underwent a currency devaluation that caused severe economic damage to the country, and we lost almost everything—but that is a whole other book!

When people ask me where I am from, I automatically respond Margarita. I lived on the island until I was thirteen, went to an all-girl Catholic school, and drove the nuns crazy. Those who know me can attest to what a waste of money that was. I spent more time in the director's office than in the classroom.

Growing up on a small island where everyone knew each other, or knew someone from your family, was a great way to grow up. The level of freedom to go anywhere without fear of others, to be able to play outdoors any day of the week without thinking something bad could happen, or to just be able to talk to anyone and feel they were part of your life, was a priceless time in my life. Then my family moved to Miami, Florida, and my life changed completely.

Since my siblings were teenagers by the time I was six, I did not have anyone to play with. My sister had moved back to Caracas to go to college, my brother married by the time he was twenty, and my other brother also moved away to college. Being the youngest (by a lot) meant that I often explored on my own. I even learned to swim on my own because both of my parents were afraid of the deep water—mostly my dad, who experienced a near-drowning experience at some point in his life. I grew up as if I were an only child. My parents were busy running their business and pursuing their hobbies (bowling, mainly), which left me alone and to my own devices. I learned to ride a bike, roller skate, swim, and pretty much any other games with neighboring children. Learning on my own at such an early age set me up for wanting to learn new things throughout my life.

By now you might be wondering what all of that has to do with the thirteen skills you need to succeed. The answer: everything. My childhood and upbringing will come up throughout this book, and knowing where and how I was raised can help you similarly identify the skills you already possess, how you developed them, and how to apply them.

Carolina Aponte
June 1, 2020

Introduction:
The Evolution of a Mindset

A skill is an ability, or some may call it a competence. Some you are born with, and some you develop over time. Your ability is a mix of what you can do, how well you do it, what you know, and the mindsets you bring that influence how you behave.

What is a mindset? According to Dictionary.com, a mindset is "a fixed mental attitude or disposition that predetermines a person's responses to and interpretations of situations." This clearly indicates that whatever mindset we adopt can determine how much success and happiness we can achieve.

Wondering how many mindsets there are and which ones you should adopt? Well, there are countless mindsets one can have, both positive and negative, depending on how you define or generalize the term. If you find yourself interested in or drawn to any of the mindsets I discuss, there is a plethora of information online about them.

The First Mindset I Adopted

Imagine being the fresh age of sixteen. You just finished your junior year of high school, and you're enjoying your summer in sunny South Florida. You're feeling on top of the world and have learned to fit in with the American kids while standing out and staying true to yourself. Now, imagine being sat down and told to pack your things because the family is moving back to Venezuela, the same Venezuela you left three years prior. You are getting ready to leave behind your high school sweetheart, your friends, your school, and the future you had envisioned for yourself in America. This was my experience at that age and a time in my life where I felt devastated and angry.

A few months later, I arrived at the airport, went through customs, and was walking to get the luggage, like my mom instructed me to do, while she went looking for the person who would take us to our next destination. Back then, you had to hire a luggage porter to walk you from the international side to the domestic side. It would be decades before you could do this without having to step foot outside.

After I picked up the luggage, I walked my barely five-feet-tall, one-hundred-pound, petite body toward the exit where my mom was, only to be stopped by an eighteen-year-old military boy armed with a semi-automatic weapon hanging on his shoulder. He told me that I was not allowed to leave unless I showed my passport—the same passport my mom took with her in the opposite direction. Since it was before cell phones, I had no way to call her in order to get my passport. I had no way to leave the airport because this boy decided he wanted to stand in my way, and the country's *machista* culture dictated that men could do and say whatever they wanted.

In a matter of seconds, many thoughts went through my mind, but the one that I will forever remember is telling myself, "I will not be staying here. I have to build my own future—one where

I'm not ruled or controlled by anyone." Eventually, I created a scene the military boy was completely unprepared for. I began to challenge him and his authority as I raised my voice and talked to others who were passing by. I questioned his legitimacy and his intelligence. I mocked him, to which he responded by threatening me with jail time. As an angry and frustrated sixteen-year-old girl, I did not care one bit what he had to say, and the more he threatened, the angrier and louder I got. Then I took a deep breath and told him that it would be a really good idea to take me to jail, that it would show his bosses what a badass he was arresting a teenager who posed no danger to anyone and just wanted to be with her mom. I told him that he would be doing me a favor by taking me out of the customs area and into a precinct because at least there, I could make a phone call to get someone to help me. Over two hours had passed, but it seemed like an eternity to me. In the end, I tired him out, and he released me to my mom's welcoming arms.

That was a pivotal moment, the moment I had the most important mindset change that would set the course for the rest of my life. At that moment, I began to develop the self-efficacy mindset, the belief that I could succeed and create a pathway to success on my own. This only meant one thing to me back then—returning to Miami, Florida.

A Promise to Myself
Life on Margarita Island had many challenges but provided valuable time for self-discovery. Many

firsts happened while I lived there, and some of those things I will share with you in the upcoming chapters. Once we returned to the island, my parents told me I had to register for school to finish my high school education. They told me I had to do it on my own because neither one of them had the time to accompany me to school, but they knew I could handle it. (Oh, so much trust in my abilities and judgment.) I took a cab to school with my file folder that contained my Sunset Senior High School records, my birth certificate, my passport, my *cedula de identidad* (equivalent to a social security card), and cash my parents handed over for the registration fees and the cab ride.

This was a private school that had been highly recommended to my parents by friends and family. The white, two-story building with big marble steps was near downtown. I walked in toward reception and was told to walk down the hall to registration. I took a number, grabbed the application that was handed to me, sat in an uncomfortable wooden chair, and began to fill out the questions and details. It was overwhelming. I had not read Spanish in several years, and my brain had switched somehow; English was clouding my mind. I did the best I could with what I knew and turned it in to the registration person. She took the application along with the rest of my school records and identification I had with me.

Time passed, what seemed like an eternity to me. I kept shifting positions in the uncomfortable chair. Restless, I stood up and walked around, drank water from the water fountain, went to the restroom, and came back and sat again. Finally, they called my name to go into the registrar's office. The registrar seemed like a nice lady; she smiled and asked me to take a seat. She shuffled the paperwork back and forth and then looked at me. "We would be happy to accept you into our school," she said. "All the paperwork seems in order, and we have space for one more student in eleventh grade." Wait, what? Why the eleventh grade? I just finished eleventh grade in Miami, so why would I have to do it again? She went on to explain to me that the classes I took in Miami did not meet the school's curriculum, and that in order for me to attend their school, I had to repeat eleventh grade to learn what I had missed by not being in the country.

I was upset—no, I was pissed! I didn't want to be there in the first place, and they wanted me to waste another year doing something I had already done? No way, Jose. I was not about to do it. I asked again if there was anything that could be done to avoid repeating a grade. Any after-school classes I could take, any tests I could take, anything? She told me there was nothing to do but repeat the grade. I got up from my seat, thanked her for her time, gathered my paperwork, and walked out of the school. I called a taxi and instructed him to take me to my brother's travel agency.

When I arrived, my brother questioned why I was there and not in school, to which I replied, "Don't worry about it. Do you have a job for me? I am bilingual, and you have English-speaking tourists.

What do you say?" He laughed, shook his head, and told to me talk to his secretary to get a uniform and register for a short hospitality course where I would learn about the island's history and geography to be able to service the tourists.

The growth mindset for self-improvement and learning all that I could to achieve my goals kicked in. Four years later, I made the decision to move back to the United States without ever graduating from high school. What does a twenty-year-old woman do in a country that is not her own, without a formal education, and with only a few thousand dollars to her name? She gets over herself and starts pursuing her dreams—first by getting a job, then by taking the GED test, and even eventually completing her bachelor's degree in business administration with a minor in accounting years later.

Growth Mindset Set in Motion

Five years into my business, Caja Holdings, I attended the National Association of Women Business Owners 2017 Women's Business Conference in Minneapolis, Minnesota, where I learned about the Goldman Sachs 10,000 Small Businesses Program (10KSB). The program assists business owners in creating a growth plan that would impact not only the business's financial growth but also the local community. I asked the program representatives what I needed to do to qualify for such an amazing program, especially after they told me the program was 100 percent free of charge to the participant.

They would cover all expenses and provide an educational opportunity based on a curriculum designed and co-delivered by Babson College, one of the top leaders in entrepreneurship education in the country. What? I just could not believe this kind of opportunity. They handed me an application, gave me a list of requirements, and off I went to my hotel room to review it and to start filling out the application online.

On October 31, 2017, I was invited to interview for the program, and on January 26, 2018, I was accepted into the program. To tell you that I was in shock is an understatement. You see, as an accountant who deals with numbers all the time, I just kept thinking, "What are the odds that out of 30 million small businesses in the US and over 800,000 in my state of North Carolina, my business would be selected?" I began the program on February 12, 2018.

Part of the program was virtual video conference classes and one week at Babson College in Massachusetts. Oh, what a facility it was! My colleagues and I experienced five-star treatment during the program, from the hospitality to the amazing meals and snacks we received daily (which of course gladly turned into a few extra pounds to carry back home). Then we came back to finish the program with one more week at Babson in May to complete our presentations and a three-minute pitch in order to graduate.

I met incredible business owners from across the United States with whom I developed not just business relationships but also a peer advisory board. If you were to hire my advisory board as coaches, it would cost you a pretty penny. By the end of the program, my growth plan was completed, and my business started providing fractional chief financial officer (CFO) services catering primarily to women-owned businesses.

This is where my growth mindset was expanded in ways I never thought possible. For both my business and myself, it represented a complete validation of the work and perseverance I had exercised all my adult life, and while I was not rich in financial terms, I could confirm I had arrived to a place I had dreamed of at sixteen. I was in control of my life, and I had clarity of mind with a business that provided financial stability and a lifestyle I truly enjoyed.

Just think about the most successful people in the world. Those who consistently succeed are those who are best at learning new skills. I know you might be thinking, "This all sounds great, but how in the world do *I* begin to develop a growth mindset?"

Developing Your Mindset

Here are the steps I recommend based on what I've seen work:

- **Start by acknowledging your imperfections.** Nobody is perfect, but we all like to think that we must be perfect in order to achieve anything. This is wrong! You just have to accept that there is no such thing as "perfection." I like to call myself *flawsome*.

- **View challenges as opportunities for self-improvement.** Be that person who finds challenges to be exciting and engaging, knowing that you will learn something valuable from the experience.
- **Replace the word "failing" with the word "learning."** Remember that when you make a mistake or fall short of a goal, you haven't failed; you've learned. Ask your trusted mentors and colleagues. Someone else can see what you are doing from a slightly different perspective than yours and may have some valuable suggestions for you. If you open up to hearing suggestions, you can more easily develop your growth mindset.
- **DO NOT seek approval from others.** I repeat: *do not* seek approval from *others*. When you do, you are actually giving up the opportunity to learn. We all waste so much energy and time seeking approval from others, even from those who have absolutely no skin in the game, that we miss the mark in learning what we must in order to grow. If there is one thing I can assure you, it's that you are the only person who will always be there for you in your life, so you are the only one you need to impress.
- **Cultivate your sense of purpose.** Having the "big picture" in mind will always steer you in the right direction. You might want to consider taking some time off to meditate or contemplate what your true purpose is. I began walking outdoors by myself early in the

morning to give me time and space to think about my purpose, my goals, and my wins and losses, which has been incredibly valuable for my growth mindset. Take the time to discover what will drive you to accomplish your purpose and goals, and then pursue it with all your might.

- **Celebrate growth with others.** If you truly appreciate growth, you'll want to share your progress with others. Watch their reactions and listen to their feedback. This will help you make improvements along the way. One way to truly grow is to listen to other's achievements, however big or small they are. They will inspire you, and you will develop a sense of gratitude for your own growth.
- **Learn from other people's mistakes.** It's not always wise to compare yourself to others, but it is important to realize that humans share the same weaknesses. If you can learn from the mistakes of others, then you may be able to make fewer mistakes yourself. And who doesn't want to save some time and heartache?
- **Once you develop a growth mindset, own it.** Acknowledge yourself as someone who possesses a growth mentality and be proud to let it guide you as you pursue your life goals.

The growth mindset creates a love of learning and a resilience that is essential for great accomplishments. Individuals who achieve great things believe they can do so by working hard, honing their skills, and learning from others, and they are persistent in the pursuit of their goals. Successful people make the commitment to dedicate their spare time in the pursuit of learning, and they stick to their promise of learning.

With that in mind, you can do countless things to learn in your spare time. In this book, I share with you thirteen valuable skills that have helped me achieve my quality of life. I believe they will help you as well, both personally and professionally. Once you have identified the mindsets that will help you achieve your goals, implementing the complementary skills is the key to your success.

In the coming chapters you will learn about the following skills: leadership, building relationships, public speaking, time management, customer service, negotiation, communications, planning and organizing, resourcefulness, financial management, problem-solving, entrepreneurship, networking, and trailblazing. As we move through each of these skills, my hope is that you gain the confidence and inspiration to begin to uncover, develop, master, and apply these skills to your career, business, or personal life and experience the lifestyle you've always dreamed.

Your Mindset Stepping-Stones

Break out your journal and write about these questions and thought exercises.

- What mindset(s) do you currently have (positive or negative ones)?
- Are any preventing you from achieving your goals and the lifestyle you dream of? If so, in what way?
- How can you go about giving up or modifying mindsets that don't serve your goals?
- Think of a challenging activity you have planned in the near future. How might you apply a growth mindset to it?
- Think of a mistake you made in the recent past. How can you learn from it? What messages will you tell yourself to view the mistake as a growth and learning opportunity?

"They happily joined me without putting up resistance or questioning my plan. That is what leadership is all about—getting people to buy into your vision, whatever that is."

NUMBER

1

Leadership

How does someone become a leader? I have read and heard over the years that you are either born with leadership skills or not. Other experts say that everyone has an innate leadership style. I agree with the latter—that we are all born with our own unique set of leadership skills; it is just a matter of identifying them and applying them to our lives with eyes wide open.

You can read hundreds of books that go into detail about the various types of leadership styles and how to foster them in a management role. That's not this book. This book is for those who feel stuck and perhaps read the word "leadership" and thought, "Oh, well, that's not me. I'm not a leader." I think you are!

If you are anything like me—and I suspect you are in some ways because you are reading this book—you have a treasure trove of memories stored in a hidden, not-easily-accessible file somewhere in your mind's hard drive. And you buried those memories on purpose, perhaps because they were painful or otherwise difficult to process at the time. I know I hid mine so well that it has taken a long time not just to find them but also to build the courage to review and share them.

Until a few years ago, I thought I knew how I'd become a leader and then an entrepreneur. Then I was nominated for the National Association of Women Business Owners Rising Star Award and had to complete a questionnaire that made me dive into the whys of my business and my success. It was hard to examine myself and my business that way! Through the process, I realized how many challenges I'd lived through, and with each one, I learned lessons and developed skills and awareness of the path I needed to follow, the relationships I needed to keep, and the ones to let go. The process of reflection was just as valuable as the award I later won and was full of "aha" moments.

I want that for you as well. To that end, I will share some aspects of my journey. My goal is to convey some of the lessons I learned to help you recall or uncover your own truths and skills to apply to your life, business, or future endeavors.

Emergence

I was an active and inquisitive child, which meant I would often get into some kind of trouble or jam, like the time I gathered the kids from my block to go explore the hills behind our houses. It was an adventure, I told them;

it would be fun to get to the top of the tallest hill, and we would be back before anyone found out we were gone. That's not exactly how it turned out.

We began our adventure around 10 or 11 in the morning, full of energy and happy to be out and about on our own. We hiked the terrain, making jokes and laughing at each other. We made it to the top of the hill for sure, but we got lost on the way down. We grew tired. Some had fallen on the rocks and had scratches, and others were thirsty and cranky. I had to rally the others to pull themselves together and then had to figure out how the heck to get us back home before our parents went looking for us. It was scary and exhausting. I did not know what to do, but since I was the one who had come up with the brilliant idea of hiking to the tallest hill, I kept my tears and fear away from my face and kept on pushing forward.

By the time we made it to my house, it was dark, and all the parents were out front, worried and upset about our little adventure. Yes, I was grounded for I don't remember how long. I was also banned from organizing any more adventures—that is until the "using the fisherman's boat as a trampoline" idea came into my head.

I didn't realize it at the time, but the hiking adventure demonstrated my natural leadership skills emerging. I had an idea. I told my friends about it with enthusiasm, describing the adventure in a way that made them want to join me. I projected a fun and exciting experience and at the same time made them feel I knew what and how we were going to do it. They happily joined me without putting up resistance or questioning my plan. That is what leadership is all about—getting people to buy into your vision, whatever that is.

The adventure went well—until it didn't. I got punished, or in other words, I failed. And of course, because I was a child, I had no choice but to obey my parents and put my emerging leadership skills to rest—at least until they stopped being upset with me and I came up with another brilliant/potentially dangerous idea.

Looking back, I can see several leadership skills in this memory: creativity, communication, motivation, confidence, and resilience. And I'm certain we all have experiences like this in our childhoods. Maybe in your case it wasn't getting your friends into trouble but keeping them out of it.

Take a moment to think back to a time in your childhood when your friends went along with an idea you had or followed you in some other way. Write it down. Did you say something to them? If so, what? What was your body language? Did you have a plan? Was there any resistance? When they went along with you, how did that make you feel? Would you do it differently now or do the same? What leadership qualities did you display? What lessons can you take from that experience to apply to your life and business today?

The Wolf in Me

When I came back to the United States at age twenty, I managed to get myself hired as a law firm receptionist. They wanted someone who was bilingual, and I was in the right place at the right time. Working as a receptionist was a great experience for me as a first real job in a professional environment. I learned bookkeeping on the old, green ledgers and was among the first in the office to learn how to use the new computers. (Yes, that is how old I am.)

Later in my mid-twenties, while working at the law firm, I knew I had to get some kind of formal education if I did not want to answer phones for the rest of my life. So I signed up to take night classes to review for the GED test. This was a challenge as I was both working at the law firm and had a second, part-time job at a retailer working some nights and weekends. I had made up my mind that I had to get educated in order to move up in life and not have to work multiple jobs to make ends meet.

Completing the GED led me to sign up for some courses at the local community college. Once I'd earned my GED and had some community college credits on my resume and experience working as an office manager for a very small import/export business, I saw an opening at a firm that developed accounting software for law firms—hello! This job had my name all over it. I started as an accounts payable clerk.

Once I got to work, I was absorbing everything around me, paying close attention to what the owner wanted, how he communicated, and what issues he brought up at meetings. I also listened to the other employees, the ones who had been there a long time and the ones who were unhappy with how things were going. (Side note: some people will always be unhappy with their jobs or their bosses or whatever; those people rarely make much of themselves. The naysayers, the overly critical people, the ones who always complain—my advice is to stay away from them the best you can! They will just bring you down.)

I began to come in earlier than most employees, before the owner got there, so I had time to get things done without interruption and could show the owner the progress we were making. I also began to "organize" the process, documenting it and getting feedback from other employees as I started writing our department's standard operating procedures (SOP). As I started asking the employees for their feedback, I began to build relationships with people from different departments. They were all eager to share their ideas with me. At that time, the company had two divisions: the software development division and the hardware division where computers and servers were built to install the software to sell to customers as a turnkey solution.

One day, at one of the staff meetings, I had built up enough courage to speak out and present ideas that were shared with me as possible solutions to some of the issues the owner, my boss, seemed to be concerned with at the time. As I spoke, I made sure to ask individuals if I was relaying their messages correctly and if they wanted to add or clarify anything. In my inexperienced mind, I felt that if I included people, pulled them into the presentation, the presentation would be more welcomed than if I tried to present it all as my own ideas and thoughts. After that meeting, my boss called me to his office. I freaked out. Had I—the youngest and least experienced person in the firm—been too bold at the meeting? I thought he was going to fire me. Let's face it—this was in the late '90s in a male-dominated business, and I was the least educated of the bunch. Everyone else had engineering or IT degrees.

Turns out, the reason he called me to his office was to offer me the management position for the hardware division. Yes, the young Hispanic woman with the least professional experience was getting a management position. Go me! The business owner told me he was impressed with how I not only knew all the issues but also got the staff to collaborate with me. According to him, the word in the hallways was that I was a bit of a "wolf." I later learned that the "wolf" leadership style refers to someone with quiet confidence and self-assurance who leads by example, who organizes and protects the pack, and who is patient and strategic. And that was exactly what the department of ten men needed! Over the years, I have developed a chameleon management style, adapting to be assertive, supportive, inspirational, or organized as the situation requires.

In this situation, I exercised leadership skills by not waiting around to be told what to do or how to do it. I engaged my coworkers and got their buy-in as I proposed new ways of doing things. Had I been a little older or more firmly "corporatized," I might not have taken the risks I did. At the time, I didn't really have much to lose and may have been too naïve to realize what was at stake. But that time in our lives has value—when we are young and eager, our natural tendencies show through.

My leadership style evolved from the adventurous kid wanting to climb up the hill with her friends to the wolf who understands that the most effective way to get things done is to share the load through collaboration and teamwork. Whether I am leading my business team to successfully deliver results to our clients or leading a group of successful women business owners in a board meeting, my current leadership style is a chameleon, easily adaptable and effective.

Developing Your Leadership Skills

Here are some tips to develop your leadership skills:

- **Be authentic.** This is the most important thing you can do because it is what will get people to relate to you and want to follow.
- **Be flexible.** We do not live in a one size fits all world; therefore, we must be able to adapt and change as situations require. You should also be sensitive to the motivations, needs and personalities of individual team members.
- **Build emotional intelligence.** Being emotionally intelligent means tuning in to what is happening in your environment and being self-aware. In other words, get out of your own bubble.

- **Ask for support.** It can be daunting at times to deal with different issues and demands. It is extremely useful to ask for support from a mentor, a coach, or a mastermind group. Talk through your leadership ideas, and identify areas for ongoing development.

One can say that the way we lead is very similar to the way animals behave in their natural habitats. What animal characterizes your natural leadership style? In her book *Wild Leadership: What Wild Animals Teach Us about Leadership,* Erna Walraven describes various animals and their leadership styles (2019). I was once described as a "wolf" because they understand the concept of teamwork extremely well. The alpha wolves are usually the ones to make decisions for the team because they know what is needed. Others refer to leadership styles in government or management authorities, such as autocratic, authoritative, democratic, and so on.

Consider what you need for your own positive leadership. The better you understand yourself, the better a leader you can become. Read some of the great leadership books out there, like Erna Walraven's and one of my all-time favorites *Dare to Lead* by Brené Brown (2018). Always remember that leaders tend to evolve over time, that different personal and work events can evoke transformation, and if you keep your eyes and mind open, you will find your own style for success.

Your Leadership Stepping-Stones

Break out your journal and write about
these questions and thought exercises.

- Describe your leadership style.
- Do you micromanage your team, not manage them
  enough, or somewhere in the middle? Observe
  and write about how your behavior impacts your
  team. How might you need to adjust your style?
- Make a list of your responsibilities and then
  note which ones can be delegated and to
  whom. Who on your team has the right skill
  sets to complete the task most efficiently?
- How do you monitor the performance
  of the people you lead?
- What is your greatest accomplishment as a leader?

"Clearly, my preferred method of communication is through the spoken word, the most common of all types even though newer generations are moving toward texting instead."

2

Communication

Have you ever struggled to get your message across? Do you sometimes wonder why someone is not responding to your expectations or requests? Or how about the unsettling feeling you got after you pressed "send" on that email to your boss? Perhaps you tried pitching a project, you were chairing a departmental meeting, or you needed to deliver a compelling presentation. You gave it your best shot, but all you received were blank looks and awkward silences.

Or—one of my pet peeves—you took the time to research before you wrote a detailed letter or email to a customer or employee regarding an issue and the next steps that should be taken, only to get a reply asking for information that was already included in your email. Worse yet, they call you on the phone so that you can explain what is already in writing. You are not alone. We live in an era where we have more communication tools than ever, yet we often do not manage to get our messages across clearly.

English as a Second Language

By now, you are familiar with my early beginnings and the fact that I was born in Venezuela, a country where the official language is Spanish. I learned English as a second language when I first came to the United States at the age of thirteen, when the only word in English I knew was "yes." That got me in trouble sometimes because I did not know what I was agreeing to when people asked me questions in English.

I started seventh grade in 1980, about the same time when the Mariel boatlift began (mass emigration of Cubans to Miami, Florida). I was exposed not just to another language altogether, but also to a new Spanish dialect. Even though Spanish is one language that is spoken in over twenty countries on the American continents, within the language are several dialects, some that I had never been exposed to. One distinct dialect is Caribbean Spanish spoken in Cuba, Puerto Rico, the Dominican Republic, and along the east coast of Mexico and Central America. It is characterized by elided middle consonants and omitted final consonants, as well as an aspirated R, which made it hard for me to understand.

Once I was admitted to McMillan Junior High in Miami, I was assigned a Spanish-speaking student as my ambassador. Her name was also Carolina, so we already had something in common. She was from Nicaragua and had come to the United States over three years prior, when her family fled the Sandinista regime. She was proficient in English and had a welcoming personality. She walked me to all my classes, introduced me to my teachers, showed me the cafeteria and the lockers, and most importantly, she told me what not to do and who to stay away from. I will forever appreciate her disposition to help me navigate the new world I was living in.

One of the requirements at the time was ESL, or English as a second language class. I was still attending all the regular curriculum classes: math, history, social studies, English, physical education, and instead of an elective, ESL. All my books were in English, the classes were all in English, and I understood absolutely nothing! I was so overwhelmed and scared that when I would go home, I would walk past my mom straight into my room, close the door, and cry into the pillow so that my mom would not hear me. I missed my house, my school, my friends, and most of all, I missed talking. I am and will always be a talker, and I felt isolated and helpless not being able to understand anything or communicate with anyone. Even sweet Carolina was from another country and used weird words in Spanish that I had never heard before.

But I was born with a certain degree of resilience that has gotten stronger with time. At thirteen, it was still being developed when the ESL teacher (who was African American and barely spoke Spanish) asked me a simple question: "Do you want to learn how to speak English?" I replied a resounding "YES." What she preceded to tell me changed my life in many ways.

She said, "The only way to learn a language is to listen to and read only that language. That means that when you go home, you watch TV in English only, preferably soap operas, because the actors will use body language in a way that you will be able to tell what they are discussing. That will allow you to connect the dots a lot faster." She also told me to listen to music in English, and what teenager do you know who doesn't like music? And of course, she told me to read the newspaper. I was able to pick up the headlines from what was currently happening in our city to increase my vocabulary. I was never a straight-A student; I had too many interests to just focus on school, to be honest. But what the teacher suggested were all things I could easily do. And I did. Within six months of arriving in Miami, I was indeed holding my own when conversing in English, and I was getting Bs and Cs in my regular classes. My self-confidence and my optimism started to come back as I began to assimilate the North American culture.

One of the things that became clear to me during this period of my life was that I needed not only to learn the English language but also to understand the culture. The more I spoke English, the more I was puzzled by why certain words I translated meant something entirely different to my new Gringo friends. For example, *ser pan comido* directly translates to "to be bread eaten" in English. A similar idiom in English would be "a piece of cake," but I didn't know that yet. The Spanish sentence would be, "*El profesor no es muy exigente, así que ese examen va a ser pan comido.*" But in English it would be, "The teacher is not very demanding, so that test is going to be a piece of cake," and not "The teacher is not very demanding, so that test is going to be a bread eaten."

Sometimes they would laugh at me, not with ill intent, but because they thought I was clueless as to what I was saying. So I began to watch other shows that were not soap operas. I watched *Cheers, The Cosby Show, Miami Vice, The Wonder Years, Who's the Boss,* and wait for it, *The Facts of Life.* Those shows gave me an inside look at what families and the general population meant when they said certain things, the colloquialisms of the Americans I was now living with.

In the end, I concluded—and try to share with any new immigrant who arrives to the United States, doesn't speak English, and feels embarrassed to mispronounce a word or afraid that they won't be understood—that one should embrace the opportunity to learn a different language, to understand a different culture, and that when you feel you are not being understood, chances are, there isn't much wrong with what you are trying to say; it's just that you need to work on how you said it.

Types of Communication

Although communication itself seems simple, often when we try to establish communication with others or others with us, misunderstandings are always possible, which can cause conflicts and frustrations in our personal or professional lives. Add cultural differences to this mix, and the window of miscommunication widens sharply.

Each of our senses have associated forms of communication. I concentrate on the following to make sure my messages are clear:

- **Verbal.** Clearly, my preferred method of communication is through the spoken word, the most common of all types even though newer generations are moving toward texting instead. We use verbal communication in one-on-one conversations, over the telephone, video conferences, and in meetings. Use a strong, confident voice so that people can hear and understand your message.

- **Nonverbal.** I have been told many times that I have no "poker face," meaning I give away how I feel with my nonverbal signs, like frowning my face, crossing my arms, or smiling. Body language is powerful, so always make an effort to display positive body language to show when you feel alert, open, and positive about your surroundings.

- **Written.** This form of communication includes writing, typing, or printing letters, symbols, and numbers to convey information. Make it simple and straight to the point to avoid losing your audience.

Reread your emails and letters before you send them to help you identify mistakes and check the tone of your message. When communicating in a professional environment, typos can make an especially bad impression, and if you are writing in a language that is not your native one, triple-check to make sure you are not committing cultural offenses.

- **Visual.** Photographs, art, drawings, charts, and graphs can also convey information. They help drive the message of your presentations and provide useful context for the audience to connect the dots.

Developing Your Communication Skills

Good communication skills improve our lives, smoothing the way in our relationships with others. On the other hand, poor communication skills can sour relationships, from business to personal, and make life significantly harder.

Some people seem to naturally know how to communicate without even trying. They can tailor their language, tone, and message to their audience and get their point across quickly and succinctly in a way that is heard. They are also able to pick up the messages sent to them rapidly, understanding both what is said and what has not been said. Some of the ways to develop your own communication skills include:

- **Listen.** Being a good listener is half the equation of being a good communicator. I have to work at this one constantly. My kids often remind me with, "Mom, did not you listen to what I just said?" I like to think it is because I have "selective hearing." What my kids and anyone else has to say is important to them, so it's important to listen, give my full attention, and watch their body language as they are talking. A little-known fact is that when someone sees you actively listening, they immediately think that you care about what they are saying.

- **Know your audience**. The way you interact with your boss should be different than how you interact with your kids or your spouse. This isn't to say you need to be a different person with everyone you interact with. Far from it. You just have to be mindful of the choice of words and body language you use. I tend to have a rather colorful vocabulary when I am in the company of friends and business associates I am close with, yet I use a less colorful vocabulary in presentations and speeches to avoid getting my main points lost in translation.

- **Overcommunicate**. You might think overcommunicating would complicate things, but really, you are ensuring that the other person understands the important parts of your message. The famous follow-up is part of overcommunicating. You want to make sure the message you shared the first time in writing or in a presentation did not get lost, and you can close the loop.

- **Simplify.** Sometimes less is more. Instead of using big words, complicated charts, and explanations, go for simplicity. You can still sound knowledgeable and professional, and you do not need to make the person receiving the message overwhelmed with details and large amounts of data that confuse them. Just provide clarity.

Your Communication Stepping-Stones

Break out your journal and write about these questions and thought exercises.

- How will your job, business, or personal life change if you develop strong communication skills?
- In what ways do your communication skills need improvement?
- What is your plan to further develop your communication skills?
- Are you a good listener? Do you give the other person enough time to complete their thoughts? Are you thinking about what you will say next instead of listening? Observe yourself and write down what you find. Do you see any room for improvement? If so, in what way?
- Do you pay attention to body language? If so, what signs do you specifically look for to make sure your message is being received as intended?

3

Public Speaking

Public speaking is one of those dreaded things
many people fear and avoid at all costs, like
spiders and snakes. It makes people sweat and gives
them anxiety and all sorts of uncomfortable feelings.
The thing is, we all do public speaking in one form or
another. We do it in the classroom when we have to
answer a teacher's question for everyone to hear, we
do it at meetings when we have to do our portions of
presentations, we do it at networking events when
we do our famous thirty-second elevator pitches, and
we do it when we pitch our services or products to
prospects. While standing in front of a large group of
people can indeed be intimidating and challenging, it is
not the only form of public speaking.

First of Many

How did I learn public speaking? Well, I learned the hard way at the tender age of seventeen. I learned by going in front of a bus full of tourists who were expecting not just to experience the beautiful landscape of the island, but also to learn the history and the culture, all while sitting comfortably in their respective seats. Keep in mind that I left the island for several years, so I had to take a crash course on the history. At the end of the tour, I had to resort to a lot of improvisation in order to get the job done. Just like Katniss Everdeen said in the *Hunger Games* trilogy, "Throw me to the wolves, and I'll return leading the pack."

That first time I stood in front of the bus filled with fifty tourists from Trinidad and Tobago, I panicked. This was an island where you naturally sweat, but I was absolutely drenched. It was not very attractive, but I told myself that I did not have any other choice and had to lead these people as I was hired to do and give them a great experience. That thought gave me the courage to begin speaking to them and telling them the history as I remembered it. I referred to some index cards I had prepared about the geography and the uniqueness of the island and its people. I answered questions as they came up to the best of my ability. And when I did not know the answer, I either made a joke about it, about me, or I told them I honestly didn't know, but I would find out when we got back to the hotel to let them know the correct answer. At the end of the tour I was thanked by several of the people, and I received compliments from others as I shared that it was my first tour. They praised me for the work I had done and the good time they experienced, and I was tipped well! As it turned out, all that sweat and anxiety was well worth it.

Rising Star

In 2017, I had the honor of receiving the Rising Star Award, granted by the NAWBO (National Association of Women Business Owners) Charlotte Chapter. The Rising Star Award is presented to a member who has demonstrated entrepreneurial creativity and determination in successfully managing a business that is less than five years old. First of all, I was shocked to have been nominated. I had no idea who thought that was a good idea. I later found out it was my favorite personal chef, Lisa! I will always be grateful to her for that nomination.

Getting the nomination was not only a shock but also a pivotal moment for my business. When you accept the nomination, you actually have to apply for the award. The application was very long, and I had to reflect on my business journey up to that point in time and answer many questions: How did the business get started? What is the business structure? Do you have employees? What services or products do you provide? What is your mission, your vision? What are your short-term and long-term goals with the business? What are the financial growth trends of the business? In other words, I had to dig deep.

The process was a bit intimidating, but at the same time, it forced me to look at my trajectory with eyes wide open. If I was going to submit this application, I needed to be honest, clear, and worthy of the award at hand.

After I submitted the application, I was selected for the second phase—getting interviewed by the selection committee. That was the most intimidating part of the process. I arrived at the interview to find five successful women business owners, some of whom I knew from networking, and then they grilled me. They had really taken the time to read my application. They asked very tough questions, and at the end, I even shed a tear or two! I am not known to be a crier, but these women made me realize at that moment, the long journey I had walked since arriving in this country at the age of twenty. I started without a high school degree, and now I own my own business and employ people. The tears were not from being afraid or intimidated; they were tears of joy, the joy you experience when you know you have achieved something important, something that impacts the lives of others.

In the end, I won the award. I was to give a thank-you speech at the award ceremony. I wrote a speech thanking my then husband for his support in helping me build my business, and I thanked my team and my fellow nominees. I kept it short and sweet. Turns out, when you win an award like this one, you are scheduled to give a *fifteen-minute speech* at the chapter's signature annual event.

I wrote and gave my speech at the event. It was shorter than the allotted time, but in that short amount of time, I was able to connect with people in a way that I had not felt before. It sparked a fire in me. Yes, I had spoken publicly many times before, but it was always about a specific topic in business and never about me personally. I never talked about or revealed much about me, but that time, I revealed part of my journey as a young immigrant woman who came to the US to pursue her dreams. And that story connected with so many of the women in attendance. Some came up to me later to ask me to share more, to give more details of how I made it happen.

I had no idea that my crazy life of trials and errors, of not accepting the status quo, of standing up for myself when others would not, of risking so much for the possibility of what I considered freedom, would connect with others. Especially in Charlotte, which— let's be honest—is a predominantly white, middle class, college-educated city, not necessarily familiar with the struggles of immigration. My mind was blown away by the feedback I received. And in turn, it made me realize that public speaking is a passion for me. That I want to do more of it. That if I can impact the life of one person by sharing my journey, then I have found my true purpose for this next chapter of my life.

That one speech opened so many doors for me, both professionally and personally. I found new friends and new clients, and the positive outcome of that one speech will always put a smile on my face. I believe it is what led me to be nominated to the board of directors of the organization, and to have been selected as one of the first five members to give a speech at the first

NAWBO Talks events in 2019. Not only was I one of five, but also I was the first one to give a speech that night. In that speech in front of a room full of people, I shared how I tapped into a pivotal moment in my life in order to let go of all the fear and to begin implementing five steps to business growth and success.

From that speech, the idea for this book was born. I talked about how each of us has a moment in life that impacts us in a way that, if tapped into, can allow us to achieve great things. That moment could lead to the growth of a successful business or just simply living the life we've always dreamed. In my speech, I talked about my return to my home country, Venezuela, and the horrible experience at the airport upon arrival. I talked about how the growth mindset played such an important part in my life to allow me to build a successful business and lifestyle.

After the speech, people came over to ask me to share more about how I had overcome the airport situation and how I had finally made it back to the US. People were interested in more details than I could share in a fifteen-minute speech. The feeling one gets when someone else is genuinely interested in your life, your journey, and your passion is validating and satisfying. It is knowing with certainty that others do care and that what you have to offer matters.

In 2018, I attended the annual NAWBO Women's Business Conference in Minneapolis, a conference that had a huge impact in my professional life. For one, I learned about 10KSB, which I mentioned earlier but will go into more detail in another chapter. Second,

I attended a breakout session on public speaking. In that one session, I learned so many tips on how to improve my public speaking: how to pause when your thoughts are getting lost in the middle of a speech, how to connect with the audience, how to calm your nerves, and how to make sure you leave your audience with a takeaway.

Public speaking can impact your career or your business. When you are able to articulate your ideas and your propositions at client meetings or management meetings, then people are able to see what you have to offer and take you seriously. If you just keep those thoughts to yourself, it is harder to advance your career or make the sale. In business, public speaking is critical to pitch your ideas to your clients, referral sources, and the general public.

Good public speaking skills are important in other areas of your life as well. You might be asked to make a speech at a friend's wedding, give a eulogy for a loved one, or inspire a group of your friends' kids to volunteer or do something positive for your community.

Over the years, I have heard many speeches and presentations, some of which have made a tremendous impact on me. Others have offered useful insights, and a few really just made me question why the person was even speaking. You can remove the fear, or at least tame it, by writing what you want to say, reading it to yourself multiple times, and recording it so that you can then listen to your own voice inflections. These steps will help prepare you to give a presentation or a speech that will not leave your audience thinking, "Why did I waste my time?" Just like any skill set, practice makes you better every time.

In the end, people appreciate the efforts you put forth, along with your honesty and your authenticity. Being a good public speaker can enhance your reputation, boost your self-confidence, and open up countless opportunities. I know it has for me, and I think it will for you.

You may be asking yourself, "How do I learn public speaking?" I say seek opportunities to speak in front of groups. Start with people you're comfortable with, like your friends and family. Talk about subjects you're really passionate about. When you talk about things you love around people you love, the nervousness doesn't kick in.

Chances are that you'll sometimes have to speak in public as part of your role. While this can seem intimidating, the benefits of being able to speak well outweigh any perceived fears.

Developing Your Public Speaking Strategies

To become a better speaker, I recommend the following strategies:

- **Plan it, write it, read it, believe it!** What do you want to say? What message do you want people to get? What is the main takeaway? Do you believe it or practice it yourself?
- **Practice.** Yes, practice not only makes perfect, but also removes the nervousness that comes with being unprepared. I recommend reading your speech into a voice recorder, then listening to it

several times. This will allow you to make changes and improvements, as well as memorize your key points so that you are more comfortable the day of your presentation. You may also want to practice the speech in front of friend or colleague; they may catch something you are saying or doing that needs to be changed to improve your delivery or message.

- **Engage with your audience.** Don't make it a one-way thing. I have found engagement with the audience to be most beneficial. Make your talk a two-way interaction with questions and participation to reduce boredom and speak with ease. Having the group involved also gives you time to reorganize your thoughts if things are going off track.

- **Pay attention to body language.** Recognize that the first time you tell a story, it won't be perfect. Take note of people's nonverbal reactions. Notice people's interest level with each sentence you say.

- **Think positively.** When we imagine a positive outcome to a scenario in our minds, it's more likely to play out the way we envision.

- **Cope with your nerves.** In other words, don't fight the fear. Accept your fear rather than fighting it because that only makes you more nervous. It's OK to be afraid; you just have to face it.

- **Watch recordings of your speeches.** Public speaking is all about refining your stories.

- **Smile.** Turns out that smiling increases endorphins, replacing anxiety with calm and making you feel good. Besides, smiling makes you look good, happy, and approachable.

- **Push yourself.** Speaking well in public can help you get a job or promotion, raise awareness for your team or organization, and educate others. The more you push yourself to speak in front of others, the better you'll become, and the more confidence you'll have.
- **Attend Toastmasters events**. Do talks at your workplace. Do a TEDx talk. Sky's the limit!

Your Public Speaking Stepping-Stones

Break out your journal and write about these questions and thought exercises.

- Does the thought of speaking in public excite you or bring on anxiety? Describe the feeling you get.
- What is your public speaking style?
- What steps can you start implementing now to strengthen your public speaking skills?
- If you get nervous, what can you do to calm down?
- What message do you want to share with your audience?

"The tears were not from being afraid or intimidated; they were tears of joy, the joy you experience when you know you have achieved something important, something that impacts the lives of others."

4

Resourcefulness

Have you ever told yourself you cannot afford to go on a vacation? Or you do not have what is needed to start your own business? Or that getting the promotion you desire is out of the question because it requires a certain degree? Or that relocating to a different city, state, or country is only something other people can afford to do. I know I have felt that way at some stages of my life. But then I think to myself, "Wait. There might be a way for me to do that. Let me think creatively for a minute, and I just might come up with a way to get it done!"

Being resourceful means knowing how to get the information and results you want. Being organized and having trusted systems are big pieces of the productivity puzzle, but sometimes getting things done means being a creative problem-solver. I have prided myself in this ability over the years. Looking back, there is so much I have accomplished without having the financial or educational resources at my disposal.

In fact, resourcefulness is always a telltale marker of an effective leader. Whether you're an entrepreneur running a business, a manager running a department, or an employee looking to get ahead, a resourceful mindset can really set you apart from your peers.

Fake It Till You Make It

As I mentioned in a prior chapter, I came back to the US at the age of twenty with just a couple thousand dollars to my name, and lots of dreams and hopes. To be honest, being resourceful at the time was really not a matter of mindset or choice; it was just the way it was for me and for most immigrants who dare to make the journey to a different country, where the language is not theirs and they no longer have support systems in place. You learn to make do with what you have, and you learn to make the most of what you do have.

So I was twenty years old with no high-school degree. My job choices were limited, and you would think I was doomed to work a low-wage service job with lots of physical labor. But for whatever reason, I thought differently. I knew a second language, and that was something not many people in the professional world had. People pride themselves in having degrees, or some kind of three- or four-letter acronym after their names that lets you know they have received some kind of educational accolade. I had none of that! I just knew two languages, Spanish and English. Turns out, that one skill was very valuable for certain types of employers, such as criminal lawyers who needed someone to translate attorney-client conversations in order to represent their clients. Suddenly, my one skill became valuable. I could use it to gain employment in a professional environment that eventually led to greater opportunities in life.

Getting hired as a receptionist at a law firm simply because I knew how to speak and write in English and Spanish made a huge difference in what my future would become. At the office, I would speak to the clients over the phone to book their appointments, sit in for the attorney-client meetings to translate, and sometimes I would go to the actual jail facility to interview the client with the attorney. The thing about being a translator is that while you are going back and forth between the two languages, the client feels comfortable enough to engage in conversation during the times when the attorney is not in the room or is handling some other matter for the client. And those conversations led to learning so much, not just about the person but also the circumstances that led to them having criminal charges. That time of my life—while I was so young and impressionable—taught me not to judge, which is something I have carried with me the rest of my life. We just never know all of the circumstances that lead people to make the decisions that they make, good or bad. The translator in me tells me that I need to keep my mind open and have empathy rather than judgment.

Who could have predicted that this one job as a bilingual receptionist would not only lead me to develop valuable skills but also teach me how to be truly resourceful? Over the years I have come across many immigrants from various Latin American countries including my own, Venezuela. These immigrants had bachelor's degrees, master's degrees, and all sorts of educational accomplishments. When left with no other choice but to immigrate to the United States (due to economic, political, or social conditions in their birth countries), they had to take on low-wage labor jobs unrelated to their fields simply because they did not know the one thing I did when I came to this country: how to speak English.

It's that simple: the language barrier is an impediment to job opportunities. It goes along with the locals' perception that if immigrants do not speak the language, then they must not be educated. (Oh, the irony.) I had the audacity to look for an office job because I was bilingual, regardless of my lack of education, and no one noticed or realized that I was (according to the workforce standards) not really qualified for the job. I was resourceful in using my language skills and the public speaking skills I had developed as a tour guide not only to get the job, but also to get my supervisor to eventually teach me bookkeeping, which would become the most profitable skill I have learned!

Relationships as a Resource

I like to think that resourcefulness is not just a means of coping with deprivation; it can also be a virtue that opens the door to greater accomplishment. For example, I made the decision to start my own business after getting fired and having a recruiter tell me I was not qualified for the accounting job openings they had at the moment. I was married with two school-age daughters, and the recession hit us hard financially. With just one income, we did not have the financial backing to start something big. Even becoming a solopreneur was a big risk, since we needed my paycheck to make ends meet. But resourcefulness is the name of the game in my house.

I searched the Internet for free workshops where I could learn more about starting and marketing a business. As an accountant, I had never really sold anything. I was always backstage and never really in front of the public. Not that I had a problem with speaking in public, but in my mind, to get clients, you had to sell to them. And that thought alone made me uncomfortable. SCORE is the largest business mentoring organization in the country. I attended one of their free workshops on starting a business. Alejandro Donoso became my mentor that day, and he provided me with the most important lesson in sales I ever learned: people do not want to hear about the product or services you have to offer; they want to connect with you through your story. "Boom, baby!" as Marise Kumar, NAWBO Charlotte past-president, would say.

So without money to market my new business, I followed Donoso's recommendations and attended all the free networking events in town, including the Latin American Chamber of Commerce, where I met Astrid, the incoming executive director at the time. We became friends, and through my storytelling, I was given the opportunity to handle the chamber's bookkeeping. In exchange, she would connect me with business owners who needed my bookkeeping services. Instead of spending money I did not have, I spent time in building relationships that eventually landed me many clients.

Resourcefulness is about optimizing what you have to work with. Innovation is not just about creating something new; it also applies to making established things work better or differently. An experienced mechanic can do wonders in car repair with a combination of after-market parts and his own resourcefulness, right? You can too, with what you have and what you already know. Not having the right resources should not stop you from pursuing your goals.

Developing Your Resourcefulness Skills

Here are some tips to develop your resourcefulness:

- **Don't reinvent the wheel.** Instead, look for a solution that someone else has already created. You might find the solution in a book, a software program, or someone's existing checklists or procedures. A world of knowledge is at your disposal and at your convenience right on YouTube. Why not use it as your ultimate resource center?

- **Rely on a powerful network.** Build and maintain a network of people you can call on for questions and support, and make sure you make yourself available to these same people when they need help from you. New networking choices like LinkedIn can be invaluable for finding more avenues and options. People from various backgrounds, fields, industries, and even age groups can provide tremendous objective insights.
- **Research and keep on searching.** Perhaps you found this book while searching for skills and mindsets, which means you most likely know the basics of querying your favorite search engine. However, coming from a tech background, I can tell you that many people do not know Boolean search techniques (such as AND/OR searches) and other ways of narrowing search results. Get a quick tutorial on YouTube on this topic. It will blow your mind how easy it is to get the information you need. Please do not forget your local library as a resource!
- **Teach others how to be resourceful too.** If your children are curious about something, teach them how to look it up themselves, and show them reference books other than just the dictionary. When your team members come to a meeting with a problem, make it part of your company culture that they are expected to also show up with a proposed answer to that problem. Make sure that initiative is encouraged.

We are all capable of showing great creativity and persistence when something is important, so make it a point to expand and practice these skills regularly.

Your Resourcefulness Stepping-Stones

Break out your journal and write about these questions and thought exercises.

- Think of something you want or need that has seemed challenging to acquire. What are alternative ways you can get what you seek?
- What are some alternative outcomes to your goal/situation?
- Who in your network can you reach out to for information?
- Who in your network can you ask for help to help you make "it" happen?
- What are five more ways to consider that would stretch my skill or confidence?

"As an immigrant, I have lived removed from family most of my adult life. My friends are my chosen family."

5

Planning and Organizing

Good planning and organizing skills allow you to manage your time and resources to reach a specific goal. It sounds simple enough, but how often do we fail miserably at it? I am guilty of all charges on this one.

How often do you say, "I meant to get to it, but I ran out of time!" We are all guilty of this. Time seems to just fly away from us, leaving us in a hot mess. The truth is that your ability to organize yourself has a major impact on your success, and it can have a knock-on effect on your team members and coworkers too.

Washing Machine Gone Bad

My daughter Gaby was home for the winter break from Boston University, where she was majoring in journalism. I sometimes work from my home office, especially if my kids are home. I get to enjoy their company while getting work done for my clients. It's a win-win situation. We had been experiencing some issues with our washing machine. The prior week it made some weird noises while my youngest daughter, Adriana, was using it, which I attributed to her overfilling the washer with too many clothes. I advised Gaby to not overfill the machine and to keep an eye on it if she was planning on doing her laundry.

In the late afternoon, as I was immersed in client work, my daughter started a batch of laundry. To give you some idea of space and location for this story, my house is a single-family, two-story home. The laundry room is located on the second floor next to the master bedroom (my bedroom) and across from my office, which is a loft. From where I sat, I could see the laundry room and the stairs. As she was leaving the laundry room, I reminded her to keep an eye on the machine. She assured me she would, and I went back to what I was doing.

About half an hour later, I stopped working and asked my daughter, "Did you check the washing machine? She was downstairs and comfortably lying on the sofa with her pup, Arnie. She replied, "No, I thought you did!" She walked slowly upstairs, and all of a sudden, I heard her screaming. I ran over to the laundry room to find over a foot of water on the floor and more coming out of the washing machine. Panic kicked in, and the adrenaline started flowing. I shouted at my daughter to shut the water off immediately. I ran to get a bucket to start getting the water out of the room. Then I called to my other daughter to get as many towels as she could to stop the water from going to other places in the house.

Gaby ran downstairs to get more buckets and yelled, "MOM, water is coming down to the first floor into our family room! What do we do?" I ran downstairs and told her to drop what she was doing, so we could move the furniture to prevent further damage. Now, we are both barely five feet tall and have no upper body strength, but that adrenaline had kicked in, so we managed to move a huge sectional sofa to the other side of the room and then roll the area rug away from the area where water was coming down. Furniture out of the way, we went back upstairs to get the water out of the laundry room and into the bathroom tub. All the while, I am thinking, "Whom do I need to call? What do I need to do to prevent further damage to the house?"

The first call I made (using Siri since my hands were full) was to Penny, the owner of a local restoration franchise and NAWBO Charlotte past president. I've known her for several years. She did not answer, but her voicemail contained the emergency number for the business. I immediately called the number and explained the dire situation we had at the house. The voice on the other side of the phone was calm and reassuring. He asked for the address and arranged for a team to come to my house as soon as possible.

The next call I made was to my insurance broker, Sal, in order to find out whether flooding was covered under my house insurance. I have known him for years and have listened to his entire joke repertoire, which always seems to put a smile on my face, so he has all my insurances: house, business, car, health, and even the short- and long-term disability. Thankfully, I was covered.

Then, I texted a whole bunch of crying emojis to my mastermind group: Trish, Hannah, and Lindsey. They are the ones who always have my back, and I know I can count on them no matter what. They all responded right away, first with a whole bunch of expletives once I sent them the pictures of what my house looked like, and then asking me how they could help. We exchanged some more texts, and then Trish called to offer whatever help I needed.

The restoration company came to stabilize the situation, with twenty different machines running to dry up all the areas affected by the flooding: laundry room, master bedroom, master bathroom, walk-in closet, guest room, hallway, and family room. Yes, one broken washing machine did all of that! My daughters called their dad, explaining the situation and asking him to come pick them up for the night. Once everyone was gone, with the insane noise from the twenty machines going, I sat in my sunroom, drank a glass of wine to compose myself, and then I drove to Trish's house to spend the night.

What does this story have to do with planning and organizing? Everything, including several skills mentioned in prior chapters. Having the ability to plan and organize is something we all possess—in fact, most of us use these skills daily. It becomes even more important when the unexpected happens. Being able to execute a plan on the go can make a difference between having only a few rooms to repair versus having an entire unlivable house to fix.

I had my contacts in my phone, easy to find. I had my relationships in a place where I did not hesitate to make the calls, even though they were not "family." As an immigrant, I have lived removed from family most of my adult life. My friends are my chosen family. I had insurance in place for all kinds of situations because no one is exempt from emergencies or life-altering events. Not only did I have insurance, but also a long-standing business relationship with my broker; it only took two rings for him to answer my call. I had a mastermind group with whom I kept in contact, even when we were not dealing with business issues. And on top of all of these things, I had mental clarity through the whole incident that allowed me to think quickly on my feet and pull out the resources I needed to overcome this unpredictable event. As my friend Trish once said, "The ability to make changes is a muscle you need to develop to manage stress." At that time, I was using that muscle just like any good athlete would!

CAJA's Plan

Starting a business is not an easy task, and that is an understatement. You have all heard at some point or another about how important a business plan is to start, finance, and grow a business. Yet a large majority of businesses never write a business plan, much less follow one. While I am wired to go with the flow to some extent, I needed structure and a plan to give me the necessary foundation to work with and make things happen. I found out that if I became a certified minority-owned business with the City of Charlotte, I could have access to a number of resources and opportunities, one being a new course at Central Piedmont Community College called Getting to the CORE of Business®. A course that would be paid for by the city and where I could learn how to organize my business and be strategic at a time when I felt so lost? Sign me up! I jumped into the course with both feet.

I walked into a classroom filled with new business owners eager to learn and implement what the course promised to do. What a wise decision it was to sign up for this course; it completely changed the way I went about creating systems and processes for my new business. Sherese Duncan, the creator of this curriculum, was and is a great source of inspiration. Her straight talk and entrepreneurial experience was very much what I needed at the time. I learned many things from her, including the phrase, "Get over yourself," as she would often call us out when we had excuses for not completing an assignment, or when we avoided telling the real story as to why we were doing X, Y, or Z. The course included vision and mission development for the business, SWOT analysis, market research, client acquisition, project management, branding elements, operating budget, cultural elements, infrastructure systems, and processes.

Each of these subjects came with a set of questions prior to getting started, a set of templates, and of course homework, which involved writing our own business details to complete the session for her to review, provide feedback, and eventually approve. I came out of the course with a binder that had a section with clear documentation and templates to handle every single aspect of my business. We have done little in my business that we are not able to replicate because the very "core" of the course was the simple concept that if you have systems and processes in place, you do not have to work as hard. And you can actually grow your business and its capacity at a scale that is both profitable and joyful.

As the overachiever (as my friends like to call me), at the end of the course, I presented my project, which was the Caja Holdings business plan and strategy. That project allowed us to almost double our gross revenue that year. Not only did I graduate from the program, but also I was invited by Sherese to become an Effició Certified Coach to help her clients develop their own plans and strategies.

Developing Your Planning and Organizing Skills

While some people plan and organize naturally, with others it takes more effort. But whether you are a natural or not, the skills and abilities you need to plan and organize a project are exactly the same. Planning a project, which could be anything from an academic project, a celebration, or a work-based job, involves:

- Knowing what you want to achieve and having a clear vision of the end result.
- Setting regular objectives along the way, so you know when you are on track or, more importantly, behind schedule.
- Making an action plan based on these objectives and arranging the resources to carry it out.
- Drawing up a work schedule or timetable, setting deadlines, and communicating regularly with others if necessary.
- Effectively managing your own time (see skill #6).

Organization skills include:
- Decision-making
- Filing
- Maintaining focus
- Proactivity
- Resourcefulness (see skill #4)
- Self-motivation
- Strategic planning
- Taking initiative

Just remember: a plan might be as simple as deciding which end of the hall to clean first, or it could chart corporate strategy for the next ten years. Small-scale planning may be easier and faster, but it is not less important. In the end, good planning skills can greatly help reduce the stress associated with today's society, make you feel more in control of your life, and help you manage your time better. And when nothing goes to plan, you can still manage how you react. Using your resilience, along with all the other skills you have learned in this book, you can handle the situation most favorably.

Your Planning and Organizing Stepping-Stones

Break out your journal and write about these questions and thought exercises.

- To become more efficient, what areas of your life need the most attention—your house, office, desk, calendar, or other?
- Would the expert assistance from an organizing company or a virtual assistant help you start organizing more efficiently? If so, make a list from your network and ask for recommendations for trusted companies.
- How much time would you gain if you did not have to search for missing things all the time?
- Which calendar format do you prefer, digital or paper? Do you schedule work and personal activities the same way? In what ways could you streamline your calendars and make them more organized?
- In your vision of success, what would a completely organized life look like for you? What steps can you take today to start making that vision a reality?

6

Time Management

Do you often feel overwhelmed by all the activities you have to do in one day and end up procrastinating? It does seem as if there is never enough time in the day. How do some people achieve so much more with their time? The answer simply lies in good old time-management, one of the most critical skills for achieving success and a high quality of life. When we have control over our time and how we get to use it, we have freedom from deadline pressure and stress.

Let's face it: we are all different, which means that my personal time-management style may not be the one that will work for you. Some of us prefer to use technology, while others like a good old-fashioned paper calendar and to-do list. What is important is that you use a system that you are comfortable with and that you can follow consistently.

Learning from a Mentor

When I was starting out with my business, I had the privilege to meet Nathan, an experienced businessman with many years as an instructor in the Charlotte area. I met him at a Latin American Chamber event, and we connected immediately. He asked me if he could stop by my office to learn more about my business, and I was more than happy to talk to him. We both felt we had lots of synergy, and before I knew it, he had become my mentor. His expertise was in time management; he had developed a system to teach people like me how to become more proficient and efficient with time management.

He took the time out of his busy day to coach me, and I started to use his method to schedule my work tasks and meetings, and to track my sales leads and goals. I blocked time not just for business-related activities but also for my personal time with my family and my kids' activities. The more I used the system, the more in control I felt, and the easier it became to say no to opportunities and events that were not a priority or would not help advance my goals.

In a short amount of time, Nathan was able to teach me a skill that is critical to success: if you have control over your time, you can achieve your goals faster and with less stress. Within the first year of implementing this skill set, I increased my business revenue by 40 percent—no joke! I was laser-focused and a lot less distracted, which meant I was able to close more deals than I had in the past.

In my own unsophisticated way, I was no stranger to time management when I met Nathan. I had developed time-management skills while working at the software company. Several years into my position as a controller, I decided it was time to get that little piece of paper that seemed to be so important to employers: a bachelor's degree. I had a great job and was making good money, but I needed the security of a degree to know that if anything were to change, I could qualify for another job at another company. Besides, I never liked being the least educated in the room. I registered at Nova Southeastern University to get my bachelor's degree. That was the only school at the time that offered night and weekend classes for adults wanting to get a higher education. It was also located only one hour away from my office and thirty minutes from my house.

I would arrive at my office by 8:00 a.m., leave to go to Nova at 4:45 p.m., attend classes until 9:30 p.m., and get home after 10 p.m. to then do homework or read the material I needed to prep for the next class. During that time, I had to schedule my time very carefully to avoid missing any deadlines at work or at school. I was working full time and had a full-time class load, after all.

This was also the time when I met my ex-husband and kids' father, Jorge. He was attending Nova as well, and we became romantically involved after I invited him to a Fourth of July BBQ at my house.

Three months later, I learned I was pregnant! So I added a pregnancy to my already-packed schedule, a pregnancy that was very much wanted but not ideally timed. My unsophisticated time-management system worked, and I was able to carry on with all that was on my plate and to bring my firstborn, Gabriella, into this world.

She did not stick to my schedule and arrived three weeks earlier than expected. Life has a way of working itself out in the end, so while I am advocating time management as one of the skills you need to succeed in life, I also want to keep it real. No matter how much you plan ahead, you need to be ready to adapt to the unexpected. Just remember to always have a contingency plan and remain flexible!

In my everyday life, I hear people complain about not having enough time to do X or Y, or that they just wish they had time to pursue their dreams but that the responsibilities of work or raising kids just doesn't allow them to do so. While all of it may sound true to them, it is most likely just a perception of their situation and not necessarily the whole truth. Most of the time, these are just everyday excuses we offer to others and ourselves to not have to face our own fears, the fears of not being equipped with knowledge, resources, and talents to go after our dreams. The good news is that we can overcome those fears when we really want something and when our mindsets are ready to make it happen. Working on developing your growth mindset is one of the most important keys to achieving your goals. Over the years, I have read countless biographies from successful people, and every one of them had multiple responsibilities and things to do, yet they made the time to do what made them successful. You just have to want it bad enough to make the sacrifices necessary to achieve your goals. I know I did, and I graduated with a bachelor's degree. That little paper is hanging on my home office wall to remind me of the time I decided that it was worth sacrificing time with friends, sleep, quiet time, and to some extent, my sanity to achieve my goal.

Developing Your Time-Management Skills

Here are a few time-management tricks that worked for me that you may consider implementing in your own daily life to stay focused on your goals:

- **Make a list or three.** Whether you prefer a notebook or to use an app, create a task or to-do lists for your personal, home, and work responsibilities.
- **Set deadlines.** Set your deadline a few days before the task absolutely must be done. This allows for the possibility that other, more urgent things will get in the way, but still allows you time to complete the task. This was most helpful with my college work, and now as a business owner, it is critical to deliver on-time work to our clients.
- **Delegate responsibilities.** Let's face it: we cannot do it all ourselves. You only have so much capacity and bandwidth, so why should you try to do it all yourself? Are you trying to prove you are some kind of superhero? Forget it! You are better off delegating the things that others can do better

than you so that you can free up your time to do what you do best. I delegated home cleaning to a professional, and that, my friend, was a game changer when I was working toward my degree! I no longer spent my weekends doing laundry, cleaning the house, and running errands to then be too totally exhausted to do homework. I delegated the cleaning and the errands so that I could do my homework and have time for my family.

- **Overcome procrastination.** Yes, this is the one thing that will set you back, prevent you from achieving your goals, and frankly leave you feeling like crap. Procrastination is one of the biggest things that negatively affect productivity. It can result in wasting essential time and energy, and it could be a major problem in both your career and your personal life.

Some tips on how to overcome procrastination that have helped me along the way are:

- **Do the hardest tasks first.** When you have the most energy and clear mind, get it out of the way.
- **Manage your environment.** If you can see temptations, you are more likely to be distracted by them. Turn off the cell phone or put it on silent mode, close out the email application, and turn off the TV!
- **Do something—anything—to get started.** Once you start, your mind will automatically drive you to complete the task.
- **Start your day early.** Most successful men and women have one thing in common—they start their days early as it gives them time to

sit, think, and plan their days. When I start my day early, I am calmer and have a clearer mind and energy to start getting things done.

Remember the many benefits of time management: greater productivity, better professional reputation, less stress, and greater opportunities to achieve life and career goals. As a result of developing your time-management skills, you will find that you are able to accomplish more of what is important. When you effectively manage your time, you feel accomplished, which is a great positive mood booster! You have less stress because you are accomplishing your tasks and goals. And as a result, you feel less rushed and face fewer problems. And how about having better health as a result of great time management? The less stress you have, the higher sleep quality you have, which gives you more time to participate in healthy activities, such as exercise and better eating habits. The other benefit that is one of my personal favorites—you only have to do things once because you are no longer rushing and stressing. And that, my friend, translates into more time for you to do the things you truly enjoy in life, such as sipping your favorite drink at leisure, or maybe soaking in a hot bubbly bathtub while listening to your favorite tunes.

The negative consequences of not managing your time effectively can lead to missed deadlines, inefficient workflow, poor work quality, and high levels of stress, just to name a few. Using a calendar to schedule certain activities or writing down a to-do list does not automatically translate into good time management. We tell ourselves that we are great time managers because we are constantly busy, going from place to place, and ending the day completely exhausted. If you are feeling rushed, it may be a consequence of either too many appointments or tasks scheduled too closely together, or you are leaving things to the very last minute without having a contingency plan in place. Then there are the poorly defined goals. If you do not have clearly defined goals, how are you supposed to know which tasks need to be prioritized? The more clearly defined your goals are, the easier it is to schedule and manage the outcome. Another consequence is lack of energy; poor time management is an energy drainer because you are either constantly chasing your tail or falling behind in tasks, which causes you to do more work to catch up! The less energy you have, the longer it will take you to get things done. And who wants to end up totally exhausted but with not much accomplished?

If you want to dive in further into time management, consider reading *Get More Done at Work* by Thomas R. Harris (2018) or, an all-time favorite, *The 7 Habits of Highly Effective People* by Stephen R. Covey (2004). Good time management requires the daily practice of prioritizing tasks and organizing them in a way that can save you time while achieving more. Use the above strategies for a few weeks and see if they can help you improve your time-management skills.

Your Time Management Stepping-Stones

Break out your journal and write about these questions and thought exercises.

- What unnecessary activities could you remove from your day-to-day life to gain time?
- Do you make to-do lists? If so, how do you prioritize?
- When scheduling time, do you include self-care and family time? If not, why not?
- What makes you procrastinate? Observe yourself and write down what you find. Where do you see room for improvement?
- Do you know how to find what your most productive time of the day is? If so, how are you spending that time?

7

Problem-Solving

First, what is a problem? For me, it is something I need to deal with, sometimes immediately (like when a washer machine breaks, and water is everywhere). Other times, you have to research and speak to parties involved to then make a determination or find a solution. Sounds like life every single day, right?

Problems arise in many shapes and forms. They can be mundane, everyday problems or larger, more-complex problems, such as what to have for dinner tonight or which route to take to work. What should I wear to the upcoming business event? How should I respond to a customer when I am running behind schedule? How should I decline an invitation without burning a bridge? The list goes on because every day we face at least one problem to solve. Regardless of what job you are in, what your family dynamics are, or how many friends or employees you have, you will be judged on your ability to solve problems. No one wants to be inconvenienced, which means you have to make life easier for others to some extent, so everyone is happy and everyone wins.

Problem-solving is important because we all have decisions to make and questions to answer in our lives.

Customizing a Solution

As a business owner, I have worked hard on improving my problem-solving skills, because it is one of the main reasons our customers sign up for our services and stay with us year after year. As an outsourced accounting and bookkeeping firm, our mission is to continuously improve our customers' ability to make informed financial and business decisions effectively. That means we must produce financial statements, stay ahead of the curve, and be able to step in when notices or urgent requests come in from our clients.

Early on my entrepreneurship journey, I met a businesswoman who was also starting her own firm, and we began to network and learn from each other. At some point, she asked me to prepare a proposal of our services to take over the bookkeeping of her young business. The day I was scheduled to make my presentation, she emailed me to let me know that she would not be present due to a pressing matter for one of her clients, but that I should still go to her office to make the presentation to her partners. She had three other partners at the time, one of them a man with a big ego.

I got myself ready, dressed the part, and had my PowerPoint ready along with my printed proposal. They welcomed me to the meeting, and I began my presentation. The entire time I was speaking, the male partner interrupted me to ask questions that would be answered by my presentation if he would have let me finish. It seemed obvious to me that he was not interested in what I had to say, and that since the person who actually knew me was not in the room, the other partners were really not interested in what I had to offer. I left the meeting knowing I would not get the contract, but I knew it was a learning opportunity for business development in my industry. Trust and credibility is what makes the sale, and I had none of it with these three partners. A few days later, I received an email from my networking friend apologizing for not having been at the meeting and letting me know the partners had decided to go with another provider.

Instead of getting upset or, as the new generation likes to say, "ghosting" my friend for not giving me the chance, I took a different approach. I continued to network with her and to refer her business and support her firm. I continued to improve the services and offers we provided to our customers and worked with my team to make sure we were on top of the issues that would come up so that our reputation as a solutions provider was a real thing and not just a marketing phrase.

A couple of years later, my friend sent me a message—"We need to talk." I called her, and we had a long discussion about the current state of her business, the changes she was undergoing, the uniqueness of her compensation structure, and the disarray of her business books. I listened carefully to everything she had to say; she had more than one problem that needed to be solved, from cleaning up the books to developing a process and a reliable system to calculate and track her unique compensation structure.

I then met with my team to discuss and get their feedback before preparing a new proposal that would be entirely different than what I had offered two years earlier. This time, it required several levels of services to solve the problems the firm was having and to manage the process in the future. Our new proposal included our standard bookkeeping services along with improvements to their accounting data collection and recording and creating a process for collecting and recording partners' contributions and distributions timely and efficiently. The pricing for these services was not even close to the first offer; this time, the solution required more time and effort on our company's part to make sure the client would get what they needed without having to dedicate so much of their billable time on administrative tasks. They signed the agreement the same day of the presentation.

I went to work, reviewed the process, the pros and cons, the people involved, the deadlines required, and the checks and balances that needed to be in place to be in compliance with both the IRS and the state board of this industry. Most importantly, our aim was to reduce the amount of time my client was spending reviewing and approving the payouts. We ended up developing a customized calculation template to record transactions in the accounting system for distributions and contributions. The solution we created and have improved on over the years is still being used by the firm to this day. The firm has grown so much that we ended up assisting in training and transitioning the bookkeeping to their own internal accounting team. But to this day, we are still a trusted consultant and advisor to the firm's founder.

Small Town USA

Sometimes we live with problems that we don't even know we have until life decides to give us little nudges that open our eyes. Such was the case over fifteen years ago while I was working for a software company. I switched job positions to have more flexibility with my time while my firstborn was still under five years old. The job allowed me to work from home some days and to travel at least once a month for no more than four days at a time. After working for so many years from 8:00 a.m. to 5:00 p.m. plus overtime, this new schedule arrangement was welcomed. The days that I did have to commute to the office were my least favorite, not because of the job, but because of the time I spent in the car commuting and the level of stress I experienced whenever traffic backed up and made me late to pick up my daughter from daycare.

One day I got an installation and training project that required traveling to a small town in Pennsylvania, outside of Harrisburg toward Newport. I arrived Sunday night as I typically would to get started first thing Monday morning. This was in the middle of summer, and the weather was awfully nice, nowhere near the humidity of South Florida where I lived at the time. I got up early, grabbed breakfast at my hotel, and drove the rental car to the law office I was to work at for the next three days.

When I arrived, I was warmly welcomed by the office manager and the rest of the staff. They showed me around the facility, introduced me to all the partners, and walked me back to the office space where I would begin setting up for installation and training. Right before I put my things down, the office manager placed her hand on my shoulder and said, "We know you have a lot to do and to teach us, but we all plan on leaving right at 4:00 p.m. The weather is too nice to stay indoors. Let me know if you want me to recommend places to visit." I smiled and told her that I would appreciate the names of places to visit while I was there. On all the trips I made for work, no one ever complained or made demands on my time as it was understood that my time at their facilities needed to be maximized to complete the project.

I ended up driving around the small town in the afternoons, visiting parks, museums, and of course shopping. Then it all hit me and hit me *hard* as I picked up a pair of jeans that cost only $7. As I paid the cashier, who was awfully nice, I thought to myself, "This is how one should live. Commute less than fifteen minutes to work. Leave early enough to pick up your child to enjoy the afternoon sun. Somewhere the cost of living was so affordable that money was not a stress factor in life." A problem I didn't know I had was revealed to me that sunny summer afternoon in small town USA. I needed a faster commute, more time with my family, and an affordable place to live in order to gain back a high quality of life.

On my flight back to Miami, my mind was working in overdrive. How could I make this happen? How can I uproot the life I had built in Miami for almost twenty years? What kind of job could I find someplace else, where I did not know anyone? What small town outside of South Florida would make sense for us to move to? How could I convince my then-husband that we needed to relocate? I arrived home, and after hugs and kisses to both my daughter and her dad, he asked me how my trip was, to which I replied, "We are moving." Of course, he asked what the heck I was talking about.

He half-joked that I drank too much on the plane. I shared what I experienced during the trip and the sort of epiphany that came out of the shopping trip. Tears fell down my cheeks as I described the feeling of peace I felt, knowing that there was a better way to live our lives rather than the way we were living it. I asked him to seriously consider what I was proposing, because after this experience I did not think I could stay in South Florida much longer without losing my mind.

The next week, Jorge came to the house with some news. He had reached out to his boss to ask if there were any relocation opportunities within the company. (He worked for a Fortune 500 company with locations in almost every state.) His boss told him there were two locations that may be good opportunities for his managerial skills: Charlotte, North Carolina, and Austin, Texas. My eyes were wide open, and my heart began racing. I had a thousand questions that we needed to research. I began researching both locations, from geography, to economic opportunities, to school ratings, to quality of life. You name it; we investigated it. We spent hours and hours researching and discussing the pros and cons of each location, which neither one of us had ever visited.

We drove to Charlotte on a Friday morning and spent the next forty-eight hours driving around town and looking at different neighborhoods we had mapped out during our research, including Indian Trail. It is a town fifteen minutes outside of

Charlotte and in a different county. Union County had great property tax rates and one of the best elementary schools in the region. A brand-new development was well on the way with beautiful two-story family homes within five minutes from the elementary school. As we drove around, we could see families walking around with their kids toward the pool and the park. There was a sense of serenity and comfort with all the greenery and open spaces. I felt the same feeling I had in that small town in Pennsylvania only a month ago.

Once we returned to Miami, the plan to relocate began to take shape. We both took on different tasks in the process. I was in charge of the budget and figuring out how to get our house sold at a price that would give us enough to purchase a new house in North Carolina and to furnish it. We also needed enough funds to support us while Jorge started his new job and I stayed home until Gaby started kindergarten. The one thing I dreaded the most was resigning from my job. I had built my career at EDSI for over ten years. They were my family and mentors. So much of my professional life was linked to this company that it literally gave me a stomachache to think of resigning.

By December 2004, less than six months after that summer trip, we had sold our house; I resigned from my job; and we sold most of our furniture, packed our personal belongings, rented a U-Haul truck, and drove from Miami, Florida, to Indian Trail, North Carolina. We were ready to begin our new life in small town USA, where I finally felt at home and no longer had to commute.

Developing Your Problem-Solving Skills

Before solving the problem at hand, you need to do the following:

- **Define the problem.** Identify the issue you are dealing with.
- **Brainstorm alternatives.** It may be mind-mapping or just talking out loud with your team, family, or friends. Sometimes the "what if" question can lead to new approaches and solutions.
- **Choose the best strategy.** Once you have carefully considered all your options, you must pick the best strategy for your problem and stick with your choice.
- **Implement the solution.** This is where you draw up an action plan, share it with the appropriate people, and follow through with your chosen approach.

A lot of the work in problem-solving involves understanding what the underlying issues of the problem really are, not just the symptoms. While dealing with a customer complaint may seem like a single problem that needs to be solved, the person dealing with the complaint should really be asking what caused the complaint. If you are able to get to the root of the problem and solve it, then the problem is not only solved that one time but also prevented from happening again.

Some of the key elements that go hand in hand with problem-solving are:

- **Creativity.** This is one of the most important skills in problem-solving because it allows us to look at things differently and to find new ways of solving problems. Intuition comes into play when you can use common sense or previous experience to make a quick decision and solve the problem.
- **Research Skills.** This may be a simple Google search or a more in-depth research project, but you need to spend the time on finding multiple sources of information to develop a strong solution to the problem.
- **Teamwork.** Let's face it: we know what we know, and we don't know what we don't know. That means that a team approach is often a great way to define and solve problems.
- **Decision-making.** These two go together because decision-making is an important part of the problem-solving process as you will often be faced with various options and alternatives.
- **Adaptability and flexibility.** With our rapid changes in technology, diversity, and society, we need to be open to new ideas and be flexible enough to work through challenging issues and to cope when things don't go as planned.

Problem-solving skills are as varied as the issues they're applied to. However, the same basic approach of identifying the problem, finding a solution, choosing the best strategy, and implementing the solution should almost always lead to a successful outcome. Remember that every problem you face is telling you that something is not currently working and that you need to find a new way around it.

Your Problem-Solving Stepping-Stones

Break out your journal and write about these questions and thought exercises.

- When in the midst of a crisis or situation, how do you identify the core of the issue?
- When you are faced with a problem, what steps do you take to identify or resolve the problem?
- How do you weigh the pros and cons before making a decision?
- When looking for solutions, do you go at it alone or seek advice? If you seek advice, how do you decide which resources to reach out to?
- What do you do in a situation when you cannot seem to find the right solution to a problem?

"She arranged an interview with her dad, and I got the job, the power of 'not what you know but who you know' in its purest form."

Customer Service

Delivering good customer service is the best kind of marketing a company can do. Lots of small businesses rely on "word of mouth" to acquire customers, the kind that comes from friends telling friends about their personal customer experience. With technology and everyone owning a cell phone, this process has evolved from sharing information mouth to mouth to posting "reviews" on various apps. I have tried restaurants, especially when I travel, based solely on the reviews I found online. If a search result comes up with four or more stars and people claim to have had the best meal and the best service at a location, that restaurant will be my first choice, and I have truly enjoyed those meals.

While good experiences usually outweigh the bad, we all have had experiences that highlight the importance of providing good customer service, not just when seeking service but also when providing it. Have you ever been to a retail store where you stood in line waiting for the cashier to ring you up and wondered why it's taking so long? Or why the store does not open up more registers? Or why the cashier has an "attitude" when you finally make it to the register? And then you think to yourself, "I should have just ordered it on Amazon!"

We all have been there with retail shops, grocery stores, the cell phone company, the student's registration office, the DMV, and the list goes on, all with one thing in common: poor customer service. Why? Clearly, the managers of those places have neglected some of the most critical skills needed in customer service. Yes, customer service is not just one skill; it is a collection of many skills!

Hostess Experience

As a young teenager I had the opportunity to work a couple of part-time jobs that involved customer service before heading back to Venezuela. Funny how lots of jobs involving customer service are left to the young and inexperienced! My very first job was as a hostess at my friend Rosita's family Mexican restaurant in Miami while attending high school. Rosita's family owned several restaurants in Mexico and had decided to open one in Miami, Florida, to keep expanding their brand. When she told me they were interviewing for the hostess position,

I jumped at the idea of making my own money and told her I was interested. She arranged an interview with her dad, and I got the job, the power of "not what you know but who you know" in its purest form.

I was quickly trained to greet the customers, to make sure the dining area was neat, all tables were set with the required silverware, napkins, and flowers, and how to assign tables to the waitstaff. At the end of the night, everyone would tally up their tips and share stories about customers and mishaps.

I was a great hostess, mostly because of my fun personality. I was always smiling and making small talk with the customers when the food was delayed so that they would not get upset. I would make jokes to keep the customers at ease, especially Friday nights, one of toughest nights of the week. All the while, I was always paying attention, not so much as a nosy person but more as a curious person wanting to learn and understand what others did.

I was paid an hourly rate and I was grateful for it; I was finally making money of my own and I could buy myself whatever kind of clothes I wanted. (Yes, I have always been in love with clothing.) But one of the things I kept hearing was the amount in tips the waitresses were collecting each night. I quickly compared that to what I was making and decided I needed a change of jobs.

Since I was a great hostess, I knew the owner was happy with my job performance. I arrived on time, I stayed as long as I was needed, I never called out, and I went over and beyond the call of duty. Knowing this gave me the confidence to ask my boss to be promoted to a waitress. At first, he smiled and he asked me if I really knew what the job entailed. I reassured him that I did and I got the job.

Little did I know that the job was 100 percent customer service. I needed to apply many skills in order to both get the job done and get the good tips! The job entailed providing menus, meeting special customer demands, taking orders, bringing food to tables, refilling glasses, and cleaning tables. All of it required patience for the customers who could not decide between one taco or the other. I needed to be attentive and pay attention to the glasses to make sure water was refilled or another beer was served.

It was important to communicate clearly to the kitchen staff as to what the customer wanted, or what changes were needed to meet their requests. I needed to have knowledge of the menu and to what was served with each menu item. Acting (yes, acting) was required at times, such as when a customer was upset over a mistake in the kitchen. I made self-deprecating jokes about myself to make sure the customer was taken care of and satisfied. At the end of each night, I counted my tips and left the restaurant with a smile on my face, because I knew exactly which new pair of jeans I was going to be purchasing that week.

Developing Your Customer Service Skills

Let's dive into the skills required to provide good customer service:

- **Patience.** This is truly the most crucial skill,

because when customers reach out to you, they are confused and frustrated and are looking for your support and guidance. You have to be willing to take the time to listen carefully to understand what the problem or need is, despite their frustration.

- **Attentiveness.** What this really means is that you pay close attention to the person or the task at hand, so as not to miss anything important.
- **Communication.** It is very important to be mindful of how you communicate. When it comes to important points that you need to relay clearly to customers, keep it simple and leave nothing to doubt.
- **Knowledge of the product or service.** Without knowing your product from front to back, you won't know how to help customers when they run into problems or demand things that you know fully well are not possible.
- **Acting.** This skill will help you maintain a cheery persona, in spite of dealing with people who are just plain grumpy. Remaining cheery and helpful usually results in better tips, better customer interaction, or even a promotion!
- **Ability to read customers.** There is such a thing as "reading the room." Look and listen for subtle clues about the customer's current mood, patience level, personality, etc., and you'll go far in keeping your customer interactions positive.
- **Unflappability.** You have to stay cool under pressure and be the rock for customers who think the world is falling apart as a result of their current problem.

- **Persuasion.** It's not about making a sales pitch, but it is about not letting potential customers slip away because you couldn't create a compelling message that your company's product or service is a valuable purchase for them.
- **Tenacity.** Call it what you want, but a great work ethic and a willingness to do what needs to be done (and not take shortcuts) is a key skill when providing the kind of service that people talk about.
- **Willingness to learn.** While this is probably the most general skill on this list, it's also one of the most important. After all, willingness to learn is the basis for growing your skills for success.
- **Empathy.** The ability to understand and share the feelings of another is more of a character trait than a skill, but empathy can be learned and improved upon. When you can't tell the customer exactly what they are hoping to hear, a dose of care, concern, and understanding will go a long way.

Just remember that customer service is an important part of every business and everyday life. Creating positive interactions at work can help ensure your business continues to draw both new and repeat customers, and help develop great relationships with coworkers. Great customer service skills are essential in your job search process and as you advance in your career, whether you apply them with external clients or internal colleagues.

Your Customer Service Stepping-Stones

Break out your journal and write about these questions and thought exercises.

- Which of the customer service skills addressed above do you feel is most important? Are there any you need to devote some time to fully develop? How do you think you need to improve your customer service skills?
- What's the best customer service you've ever received? What made it so special?
- Have you ever received negative feedback from a customer or boss? What did you do with that feedback?
- How well do you know your products or services? Describe them.
- How would you define good customer service for your own job or business?

9

Building Relationships

Relationships are my Achilles' heel. Building positive relationships was one of the most challenging skills for me to develop and understand. Relationships come in all sorts of shapes: family, romance, business, friends, networking, academic, and more. We spend a lot of our energy on these relationships and must deal with all kinds of feelings.

How many times have you told yourself, "That's it—I am not answering her call anymore," or "They always make me feel bad about my choices, but they are family, and I have to spend Thanksgiving with them," or "This pompous jerk thinks he knows more about my job than I do, and he just got here the other day," or this one, which I have thought many times, "I am going to need a glass of wine to be able to get through this meeting with Mr. Know-it-all"?

Relationships can be complicated, but they can also be amazingly easy. We do not live on isolated islands. We are constantly surrounded by people and must make our best efforts to build the right kinds of personal and business relationships in order to achieve life balance and success.

Love Being in Love

Let's just say that as a Pisces, I am forever in love with love. At my current age, I can categorically say I have been in all kinds of relationships—some good, some bad, and some that were necessary for me to grow. A friend told me recently, while we were discussing this book, that I could easily write another book on the love topic alone.

While working as a tour guide, I met many different types of people and even dated some, including the guy who would become my first husband, Carlos. He was native to the island, a son of a well-to-do family who, like me, had lived in the United States. He actually attended a military school in North Carolina. (What a small world since I now live in North Carolina.) When he finished high school, he returned to the island but did not register for college in Venezuela. He had a falling-out with his father, moved out to a small studio apartment, and started working in the same company where I was working as a tour guide. He was good looking, fun, and just like me, did not have a great relationship with his parents and wanted to return to the United States. One would say it was meant to be. We were at the right place at the right time!

Once I set my eyes on Carlos's smile and good looks, I could not help myself; I had to do something about it. As tour guides, we wore the official shirt and hat with the company logo, and we were allowed to wear pants, shorts, or skirts, and whatever type of shoes we felt comfortable in. I almost always chose to wear jeans and tennis shoes if the tour did not involve a stop at the beach. If we were going to the beach, then I chose to wear Bermuda shorts and sandals. But whenever I knew he was going to be on the same scheduled tours, I chose to wear shorter shorts to display my curves and my tan legs. I also began wearing a bathing suit top, so I could open my shirt on the beach tours and give him a glimpse of my assets.

He took notice, and we hit it off and began our romance. At this time, I was already very independent. I was paying rent, giving food money to my parents, and coming and going as I pleased. No one was questioning my whereabouts, which meant that I spent most of my free time with Carlos. We had long conversations about our experiences in the US, shared our dreams, and were intimate in other ways. (This was a hot island, we were young, and there was no Netflix.)

One day, while sharing those dreams, we started planning how we would return to the States. That plan required us to get married because of our age. I had to wait to turn eighteen so that we could apply for the visa to get to the United States legally. By showing that we were married, had a rental property, and steady jobs, we were able to get the visa to finally go on our "honeymoon."

Getting a visa to come to the United States is not as easy as those who are born in the US believe it to be. One has to go through a lot of red tape to qualify for a visa, so sometimes people like me have to get creative to get to where we want to go. The immigration system is way too complicated and should be brought into the twenty-first century. I digress.

We met with my parents to tell them that we had decided to get married, and there was no opposition. In fact, I believe my parents were relieved that I was getting married and was no longer their responsibility and wouldn't be living under their roof. I just think that they were at a stage in their own lives where I was just no longer a priority.

We decided on a small, simple wedding; we did not want to spend money on an event that was simply a means to an end. The romantic worldview of a wedding with the long, white dress, flowers, hundreds of guests, and a party to die for was not our view. Marriage was, in fact, more of a strategic decision on both of our parts to get what we wanted. After the wedding, we moved to a little house near the beach and began working multiple jobs in order to save money for our trip to the United States.

We announced to the family that we would be traveling to Miami to attend my sister's wedding, representing the family who could not attend. My parents' financial crisis continued, so they were happy to know I was going. We traveled to Caracas to get our visas, and we purchased airfare tickets to Miami, Florida. We started discreetly selling things that we owned, such as furniture, cars, and jewelry. We knew we were not coming back, and we didn't want anyone to ask questions.

When we got on the plane, we looked at each other and smiled. We were on our way to a place where we were going to build our dreams and experience the freedom we never really felt in our own country. We arrived in Miami and stayed at my sister's apartment to help her with the last-minute preparations for her wedding. While attending the wedding, I met a Venezuelan man named Gustavo. He asked me what my plans were, and I flat-out told him my plan was to stay in the US and that I needed a job. He said, "My roommate works for a law firm, and they are looking for a bilingual receptionist. I can get you an interview if you'd like."

The following Monday, I went to the interview and was hired on the spot. That job changed my life. It was where I learned bookkeeping, and I was fascinated. I felt a sense of accomplishment that I had not felt at any of my previous jobs. I knew then that I would pursue accounting as a career. (I still didn't even have a high school degree!)

Once we were both in Miami working and trying to build our new lives, the romance we felt for each other fizzled away. The reasons for us to be together no longer applied. We were so young; I was twenty, and my memories of the airport when I was sixteen came back strong. I began to question why I was really married, since I had done so many things to be able to gain freedom in the United States. The problems started right away, and at the time, I had no patience or desire to work things out, so we parted ways. There was no harm done as far as I was concerned. We had no kids and no assets. We could just move on with our lives independently, so less than a year into our new life in Miami, we filed for divorce. I was finally as I was always supposed to be: free.

The Right Kinds of Relationships

As I mentioned in a previous chapter, I worked at the law firm for several years until I outgrew my position and overstayed my welcome. I applied for an office manager position at a small business in Miami, Florida. This job connected me with a Venezuelan businessman, Miguel, who used to be a banker in Venezuela. He ran the IT department for one of the largest banks in the country, and that gave him the opportunity to travel the world, earn financial freedom, and open his own business.

We met at a professional business meeting; he was doing business with my boss at the time, and I had to get some information from him in order to prepare a bill of lading. I was dressed in a business suit, one that gave the impression that I was all business. I began asking him questions about his business, which was based out of Venezuela, and he told me that he was in the process of moving to Florida and wanted to open an office in Miami. He asked me lots of questions about my job, what I did, and what I knew, and our conversation turned into an interview for a job in his new office in the US.

Truth be told, I was not happy with my job at the time because the owner was a bit weird. He would disappear for days at a time without checking with anyone at the office. His business finances were not great because he kept drawing money to renovate his home, and he had married this very young and beautiful woman whom he wanted to impress, but I digress. When Miguel presented the opportunity to work for him and help set up his office from the ground up, I jumped at the opportunity.

First, I focused on finding an office space and learning about leasing agreements, which led to learning about business registration, LLCs versus C corporations, and what permits and registrations were required based on the type of business, in this case an import/export business. Then I acquired furniture, computer equipment, and a phone system. I was responsible for the letterhead, logo, website, business cards, the accounting system (no more green ledgers), putting out job ads to hire employees, training new hires, negotiating with vendors, responding to clients' demands, and the list goes on. I learned many things about running a small business, from A to Z, and wore many hats even though I was not the owner. I thrived on the challenge.

That job lasted for several years. Miguel became a mentor to me, and his family became my family. His wife at the time was a lovely woman who was also a great cook and entertainer. He owned a yacht and invited me frequently to join them on the weekends to go sailing around the coast. Those weekends were priceless to me, not only because I love the ocean, but also because we engaged in interesting conversations where he would share with me his business experiences and goals, and sometimes we had strategic sessions while sipping wine and watching the sunset.

When his business underwent financial difficulties due to the economic crisis in Venezuela and other Latin American countries, he told me that as much as it pained him to see me go, he just could not afford to pay me what I was worth. He wanted me to be in a position where I was secure financially and would be able to grow and shine. He remained a mentor to me for many years after I left that job.

Business Sorority

Over the years, I have managed to develop many types of relationships, some successfully lasting many years. I am really good at building relationships with business associates, employees, friends, and nieces.

For example, I developed a strong business relationship with my mastermind tribe, women who later became friends and confidants. As I mentioned earlier, my siblings were not around much when I was growing up because of the big age gap between us. My parents were doing the best they could with what they knew, so they were not around much either. And because I moved from one country to another multiple times, it was hard to maintain or develop personal friendships. I did not finish high school, nor did I attend college. I got my GED at the age of twenty. I was never in a sorority or other collegiate women's groups. I operated solo. Me, myself, and I.

A few years ago, I met Mel while serving on the board of a nonprofit organization. She is a rock-star financial planner with a personal mission of gathering like-minded women to support each other in different areas of their lives. We liked each other right away, and she invited me for coffee to get to know each other better. While sipping coffee and asking me lots of questions, she pitched me her networking group, Business Sorority. I immediately put up my wall. I mean, a group of women getting together regularly just gave me the hives. I personally dislike gossip and cattiness; I could not even attend the PTA at my kids' schools because I just could not stand listening to the moms talk about other moms or their ridiculous, unrealistic expectations of what a mom should be or do. I never felt I had anything in common with those moms. As a mother of two daughters, I told them early on that I was allergic to "drama" and that it was best if they did not bring drama home so that mommy would not get sick with hives and hyperventilate! It worked for the most part, at least until they became teenagers. Then it was game over.

Mel invited me to a Business Sorority meeting. I was unsure, so I told her I would think about it and check my calendar. She did not pressure me; she just said she would include me on the email list for event announcements and that I would be welcome whenever I was ready. After several months, I caved and attended a luncheon. I enjoyed the speaker and met some interesting women who did not strike me as gossipy or chatty. On the contrary, they were smart, business driven, and welcoming, and I was pleasantly surprised. I was invited to join the group, so I could participate in the many events and opportunities they had for members, one of them being the mastermind group. That caught my attention.

In July 2016, I officially joined Business Sorority. As with everything I have done in my life, I went all in. I truly believe that is the only way to obtain the best results. If you do anything halfway, then you end up with poor results. So when the mastermind group season opened up, I attended the meeting and joined a group.

We started out with eight members, but as the meetings progressed, some dropped out and left four, which was a perfect number. Trish, Lindsey, and Hannah are all very different; we have different businesses and careers, different backgrounds and family dynamics. Yet we have built a strong bond over our mastermind meetings, where we share business and career challenges and personal (and I mean very personal) issues. Through it all, we are each other's biggest cheerleaders and encouragers.

We are also the biggest truthtellers—no BS allowed. We force each other to truly listen to ourselves and see the barriers we put up to ignore the face of reality. We keep each other honest and accountable to the goals we set for ourselves. This is my tribe, the ones I know I can call on at any hour of the day with a simple text message that says, "Can we meet for a glass of wine?" We know what that really means: we need someone to listen to us without judgment, and to help us see what we are not able to on our own. It means knowing you have someone who has your back unconditionally. You can only build this type of relationship when you are able to be honest, vulnerable, and most importantly, your 100 percent authentic self.

Never in a million years did I imagined that joining a women's business group would have such a positive impact in my life. I have Mel Miller to thank for that. While this book was being edited, cancer took over her body. She fought a good fight, just as she did with everything in life, but ultimately Mel passed way. I will forever be grateful for her influence in my life.

Developing Your Relationships

Here are some tips to help you develop positive relationships:

- **Be your authentic self.** Phoniness can be spotted a mile away and can actually prevent you from having great relationships.
- **Pay attention to the whole person you are trying to build a relationship with.** Listen to their words, but also watch their body language for

clues that indicate what is important to that person or what makes them uncomfortable.

- **Accept and celebrate differences.** We always feel more comfortable when we are with people who think like us or act like us. But the truth of the matter is that you cannot grow as an individual unless you experience and accept the challenge of listening to a different point of view or being open to a different way of doing things. In any case, life would be very boring if we were all the same.

- **Be intentional with your time.** Time is a limited resource, so giving your time to people is a priceless gift. Use your time wisely, so you can be available when loved ones, friends, and work colleagues need you.

- **Develop empathy.** This is such an important key to building relationships. This is the state of perceiving and relating to other people's feelings and needs without blaming, giving advice, or even trying to fix it. While she may not have been first to utter the sentiment, Maya Angelou once said (and I think she said it best), "People will forget what you said, people will forget what you did, but people will never forget how you made them feel."

I do have to add a caveat to building relationships: try to have a positive self-relationship before you begin any new relationship, personal or business. You are with yourself more than with anyone else, and while we hear mixed messages about self-care and self-worth, you do have to love yourself—heck, like yourself—before pursuing new relationships. Every relationship can teach us something and can lead to a happier, more fulfilled life.

Your Building Relationships Stepping-Stones

Break out your journal and write about these questions and thought exercises.

- List the top five closest relationships you have. How do each of these relationships fuel you toward success?
- For fun, list the favorite food, color, and TV show of your closest five friends or family members? If you don't know, enjoy the fact-finding mission to get the answers from them.
- Do you spend time on your self-development and personal awareness each month? List the two biggest things you've learned about yourself recently.
- Describe the different types of relationships you have in your life. Are any types of relationships missing? What steps will you now take to build or attract those relationships?
- List things you do that help you to be a good listener. How could you become a better listener?

10

Networking

Networking is a dreaded activity for some, especially if you are an introvert. The action of interacting with others to exchange information or develop a professional relationship is daunting, even for extroverts like myself. Have you ever uttered the words, "I hate networking," or asked yourself, "Is this even worth my time?" Have you just felt uncomfortable and phony after attending a local networking event?

The first thing that prevents us from building a strategic network is the mindset that networking is self-serving. A strong network, however, is built with mutually beneficial relationships. In the process of getting to know someone, you understand how you can add value and help them, and in turn, they are willing to help you.

Depending on what part of the world you are from and what profession or business you are in, networking is often a necessity in the business world. Tons of studies demonstrate that professional networks lead to more jobs and business opportunities, increased knowledge and skills, and an increase in job satisfaction, just to name a few benefits.

Even though so many people feel awkward or uncomfortable when one mentions the word "networking," the fact of the matter is that we all do it all the time without even realizing. When you were a kid, you networked with the kids in your classroom, especially during recess on the playground. When you were in high school, you networked with your classmates, or teammates if you participated in any kind of sports. You networked in your neighborhood with the other kids your age and their siblings. When you start a new job, you have to get to know your coworkers, managers, customers, vendors, and so forth. Those are all forms of networking you participate in without realizing it.

Building My Network

Today, I can proudly claim to have a network of business associates, clients, and friends that spans multiple states within the US and other countries. How did I make it happen? It all started the month I decided to go into business for myself. Now, I am no introvert, and the time I spent as a tour guide prepared me to have no shame or qualms about talking to strangers. As my oldest daughter once said, "You have never met a stranger, have you?" Engaging in conversation comes naturally to me. Since all human beings have something in common, there is always something to talk about.

There are, however, times in our lives when opportunities to meet new people or engage in conversation with strangers are limited. Such was the case prior to starting my business.

I relocated to Indian Trail, North Carolina, in December 2004 with my then-husband and my oldest daughter, Gabriella. We made the bold decision to leave Miami, Florida, where our family, friends, and everyone we knew lived, seeking a better family lifestyle and educational opportunities for our daughter, who was four years old at the time. We did not know one person in the area, but we were not intimidated or concerned. We are both immigrants and very familiar with the process of leaving the comfort of the familiar to venture into the unknown.

The first year in North Carolina, I did freelance software support and accounting out of my house, while Jorge went to work at a warehouse. That meant that I did not have many interactions with people other than the parents (mainly moms) of the kids in my neighborhood, and to be honest, I did not feel any inclination to socialize with these women. I found we did not have much in common other than being parents. They wanted to be in the PTA, and every activity was related to kids. Although I love my kids, I have a life and thoughts outside of being a mom. I kept those networking opportunities to a minimum, and at the end of that first year, it took a toll on me.

I was craving adult interaction and the intellectual stimulus that came with it. So I did what I had to do to get out the house: I got a job. I applied to several accounting positions until I landed a job with a multistate flooring company. It was a growing business that needed someone with my software skills and ability to convert their accounting system to a new platform. I was thrilled to be back to work full-time and surrounded by other adults. I began to build friendships and business connections.

While working there, I became pregnant with my daughter Adriana. It was a very difficult pregnancy. I was forty years old, I was sick pretty much the entire time I was pregnant, and the heavy workload took a toll on me. Adriana decided to show up at only thirty-two weeks, way too premature. I had preeclampsia and had to have an emergency C-section to save my daughter and myself.

After the birth of my daughter and my challenging recovery, as I was having all kinds of health issues, my employer decided they could not wait for me any longer and let me go. The timing sucked, but such is life, and you move on. Another job came but with fewer opportunities for me to be around people, and with two kids at home, my adult network was shrinking again. That is until I decided to start my own business and had to intentionally build my network.

I signed up for every free business workshop and networking event there was. I began intentionally setting up one-on-one meetings for coffee or lunch with people I found interesting, not just people to whom I could sell my services. I read somewhere that it's not what you know but who you know that will get you places, just like my friend Rosita made it possible for me to get my first job as a hostess at her dad's restaurant. And in business that does seem to apply. I began building relationships with individuals who seemed to be involved in the community, who had been in business for a while, and who offered to connect me with others they thought would be good contacts for my business. Soon enough, my calendar was full. By day, I was out meeting people and then spending afternoons with my kids on their homework and activities. By night, I was doing the work my clients paid for. It was crazy and exhausting. At the same time, it was encouraging and exciting, and I found more opportunities than I anticipated.

One of the opportunities was to lead a new referral networking group called LeTip, similar to Business Network International, or BNI, where you meet regularly and provide a business referral to someone in the group to help grow each other's businesses. I jumped at the opportunity to be involved in leadership and connecting people with each other. Amira Issa, a financial advisor, and I were the founding members, and after a year of nurturing the group, we grew to over thirty-five members and countless visitors. It was a very rewarding time, where I met great people, learned the art of networking intentionally, and expanded my network beyond what I thought possible.

In one of my speeches for NAWBO Talks, I mentioned the importance of building relationships with community connectors. We've all gone to an event, had the wine, and exchanged business cards with at least five people, only to drop them into the growing pile of cards in our desk drawers. In order to grow your business or career, you have to do more. You must actually get to know those community connectors personally. Make time to show up to support them and thank them for their support and referrals.

I learned how to implement a referral system that works for my business from one of my clients, Stacey Randall, and her "referrals without asking" system, which includes identifying your referral sources, creating a follow-up process, building for the long term, planting the seeds, and one of my favorite parts, automating (Randall 2019). It helps ensure that our sales pipeline always has prospects and that my business maintains long-term relationships with both clients and referral sources.

Believe me: I understand that when the calendar is already overcrowded with work and family commitments, the last thing you want to do is make small talk with strangers. However, the power of a strong, professional network can have such a positive impact on your career or business, and when done well, networking will give you a competitive edge.

Developing Your Networking Skills

Here are some tips to improve your skills to ensure you're networking efficiently and effectively:

- **Determine what networking style is for you.** Whether you are attending a large event, such as a gala or a chamber of commerce luncheon, or a one-on-one over coffee, figure out what is most comfortable for you and do it as many times as possible.

- **Network outside of the norm.** The truth is that you don't have to attend the traditional cocktail party in order to be a successful networker. All you have to do is find an event or opportunity where you can meet people with common professional or personal interests. You can achieve great networking contacts even while volunteering.

- **Make a plan.** While you don't need to know exactly what you expect of each networking opportunity, it's important to head into each activity with a goal. For example, you may attend an event with the goal of connecting with three new people in your industry or bringing back one new insight to share with your coworkers.

- **Follow up.** Sounds simple and easy to do, but so many people fail miserably at it. After you connect with someone, you must follow up by either writing an email, connecting on LinkedIn (which is less personal), or handwriting a note. Whichever method you choose, remember to make it personal. We are all hardwired to respond well when we feel like someone listened and cared about what we had to say.

- **Pay it forward.** In my view, this is the most important aspect of networking. You must provide value to those in your network before you ever ask for anything. This means you must show up and support people both professionally and personally without being asked to do it.

Many of us, if not most, are ambivalent about networking. We know that it's critical to our professional success, yet we find it taxing and often distasteful. By implementing the above strategies, you can overcome your aversion to networking. By identifying and exploring shared interests, expanding your view of what you have to offer, and motivating yourself with a higher purpose, you'll become more excited about and effective at building relationships that bear fruit for everyone..

Your Networking Stepping-Stones

Break out your journal and write about these questions and thought exercises.

- What's the biggest thing you're working on at the moment that could benefit from a powerful network?
- What is your thirty-second elevator speech about yourself and your company?
- What questions do you ask to engage others while you are networking?
- How do you track your connections?
- How will you follow up with new connections?

"If you're a business owner or leader, you need to know how to negotiate. If you are a parent, negotiating is nonnegotiable."

11

Negotiation

Negotiation is not just a skill relevant to dealmakers. In fact, we negotiate almost daily without even realizing it, such as where we want to eat for lunch, how much time we should spend on a project, or how much to pay our kids for household chores. We have these micro-negotiations with ourselves and others all the time.

Just think of all the times in the week you negotiate with new hires and existing employees, with sales prospects and long-term clients, or with vendors and suppliers. If you're a business owner or leader, you need to know how to negotiate. If you are a parent, negotiating is nonnegotiable!

Overseas Trip

What I've learned about negotiating is that you must come to the table with something the other person wants, and you must be able to sell it in a way that the other person understands and appreciates what you're offering.

I once convinced my parents to let me go on a school field trip for twenty-one days to Spain and Italy. The nun who founded the school I attended was becoming canonized at the Vatican, and they organized this incredible trip that gathered students and people from all over the world. I was ten years old when I attended the Beatification of Santa María Rosa Molas at the Vatican, Italy, by Pope John Paul II on May 1, 1977. I urged my parents to allow me this once-in-a-lifetime experience because it would be good for my education. Since I was the youngest of four and they were busy running their business, they happily agreed to send me off with the nuns.

It was a fabulous trip with so many sights to see and so many things to do, but I was ten and spending time with several of my school friends, which meant we were acting up at some point or another. The nuns would use scare tactics to keeps us in our rooms at night by telling us there was a rapist in town (yes, they actually said that) and that we needed to stay in our rooms with the doors closed to be safe.

One night, a few of us were hanging out in my room chatting away and making fun of the outrageous stories the nuns told us throughout the day. We were also very interested in the cute Italian boys and the waiters at the hotel. I was a precocious child and was starting to go through early puberty, which had my hormones all over the place. We decided that we should act out a scene as if the attacker were coming for one of us, to see what we would do and how we would react. I told my friends we needed to be ready in case any of us encountered the dreaded man we were warned about. We set the scene and started laughing when the "attacker" pushed me hard. I fell down and hit my head on the corner of the night table, which left me bleeding profusely all over the bed before I fainted.

Everyone panicked, and one of the girls opened the door to call the head nun. Everyone else fled to their rooms and left me there, bleeding. The nun came running, got me up, and took me to the hotel's nurse. She determined that I did not need stitches but needed to rest the next day. No tours for me. They told me they had to call my parents to let them know I injured myself, and I begged them (or better yet, negotiated with them) not to do that. I told them that my parents would be terribly worried and would most likely blame the chaperones for allowing me to play with my friends after hours, and with so many days left on the trip, what would be the point of alarming them when they could not come see me? This was pre-FaceTime after all. I offered to be on my best behavior the rest of the trip. I said that I would be a model student because this experience taught me a valuable lesson, and wasn't that one of the outcomes they wanted for all students, to learn and better themselves? Ultimately, they did not call my parents, which was the beginning of many negotiations I would navigate with my parents and my teachers throughout my childhood and into my teens.

Tour Guide Gig

When I was seventeen, I became a tour guide in my hometown of Porlamar, Margarita Island. The pay was not great, so I made up the earnings with tips and commissions. As I gained experience on the job, I learned that since I lived on an island that was a duty-free port, tourists expected the tour buses to visit the best shopping areas. I also learned that some of the shop owners gave a percentage of the sales to the tour guides as a commission for bringing the tourists to their shops.

In a place where there are literally hundreds of shops with very savvy and shark-type owners, I learned to negotiate with the store owners for not only a higher commission, but also the best conditions for the tourists to have the best experience and treatment by the staff. In order to make more money, it was crucial to make sure the tourists did not feel hustled. I made sure the negotiations with the store owners provided the most favorable outcomes when my bus stopped at their stores.

I talked to the store owners, knowing I had plenty of other stores I could choose. My strategy was to build a rapport with the store owners, so they liked me and felt that it was a good deal for both of us. Ultimately, I wanted to make sure my clients (tourists) had a great experience because that would increase my odds of getting good tips and referrals.

I also learned to negotiate the kinds of jobs I wanted to get from the tour company. The company gave full-day tours, half-day tours, nighttime tours, and a private island day tour. I learned logistics and the history of the island and the experience the tourists were looking for. I also learned the types of tourists that were the best tippers. The private island day tours were where the most money was made. The tips were way better in these smaller tour groups because of the personal connection you could build.

At some point, I started asking my clients to put in a good word for me with the travel agency. Once I received some really good reviews, I requested to be assigned to the private island day tours. During these tours, I drove a vehicle with no more than four tourists at a time around the island, pretty much deciding where and what we were going to do for an entire day of sightseeing. Thanks to the negotiating skills that I learned when dealing with the store owners, I applied the same tactics with the restaurants we visited. During an all-day tour, I drove the tourists to beautiful locations and arranged for delightful meals by the water and a shopping trip for great bargains. We closed out the day with a beautiful dinner at a popular bar or restaurant. When I dropped off the tourists at their hotels, I collected great tips in US dollars, rather than the Venezuelan currency, a big win for me.

Developing Your Negotiation Skills

You have undoubtedly encountered one or more of these types of negotiations: asking for a raise (or setting a salary if you're the boss); finding an agreeable time for a vacation or leave; terminating an employee; discussing a change in work schedule for an individual or team; writing contracts for unions, suppliers, freelancers, or consultants; deciding which movie to see or where to go out for dinner; planning how to spend your household budget; setting a rate with a vendor or customer; and so on. There are typically four stages of negotiating: preparation, exchanging information, bargaining, and closing the commitment. The main strategies you need to improve or build up your negotiating skills are:

- **Set your goals for the negotiation.** What's the best possible outcome? What's your bottom line? What's your plan B?

- **Believe in the value you bring.** Going into a negotiation knowing the value you deliver will give you the confidence to advocate for yourself. This means you need to do your research and know the facts.

- **Build rapport.** Engage in small talk at the start of a negotiation. If you spend even just a few minutes getting to know each other, your conversation may be more collaborative, and you are more likely to reach an agreement. If you're negotiating over email, even a brief introductory phone call may make a difference. This is one of the most valuable negotiation skills to master. People like doing business with people they like!

- **Listen actively.** Once you start discussing substance, resist the urge to think about what you're going to say next while your counterpart is talking. Instead, listen carefully to their arguments, then paraphrase what you believe was said to check your understanding. Acknowledge any difficult feelings, like frustration, behind the message. This is where empathy plays a big role.

- **Pay attention to body language.** One of the most powerful tools for any entrepreneur sitting at the negotiating table is the ability to read and interpret body language—subtle gestures, movements, and expressions can speak volumes about what the other person is thinking, and more importantly, whether things are going well or on the verge of breaking down. And if you are negotiating with your spouse or children, their body language will most definitely give you a clue as to what their minds are really focused on.

- **Call on your problem-solving skills.** As mentioned previously, a lot of the work in problem-solving involves understanding what the problem's underlying issues really are, not just the symptoms. Once you identify the underlying issues, find a variety of solutions.

- **Create a plan of action.** Another way to improve the long-term durability of your agreement is to place milestones and deadlines to ensure that commitments are being met. This always gives a sense of security to the other party.

- **Play fair.** A quick win with lower costs is great, but if you always negotiate below cost, you could damage your reputation or receive poor quality of service, which ends up costing you more in the long run. As the saying goes, "You get what you pay for."

In the end, negotiation is simply a method of getting people to come to a mutually beneficial agreement while avoiding conflict. Being a good negotiator requires a set of skills and knowledge to make sure that the required objectives are reached. Learning how to be a better negotiator means you won't have to pay the price for the alternative. The more knowledge you possess of the issue at hand, the greater your odds in successfully getting the other party to agree to your request or proposals.

Your Negotiation Stepping-Stones

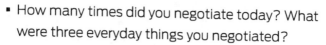

Break out your journal and write about
these questions and thought exercises.

- How many times did you negotiate today? What
  were three everyday things you negotiated?
- How can you improve your negotiation
  skills? What skills do you need to add
  to become a better negotiator?
- What steps do you use when negotiating? Are
  you clear on your negotiation goals? Do you
  have a strategy when going into a negotiation
  meeting? If so, what does it look like?
- Do you know the value you bring to the table?
  If not, what can you do to figure it out?
- What kind of mindset should you have to
  become an effective negotiator and why?

12

Money Management

The financial sector has a saying: cash is king. Typically, it means that cash is superior to stocks, bonds, annuities, property, and other types of investment, particularly during certain fluctuations in the market. What it means to me is that cash is a means to an end.

How many of us have struggled financially and still do? How about ignoring the pile of bills on top of the kitchen counter because looking at them just gives you more anxiety? According to the US Census 46.75 percent of US households earn less than $50,000 per year, which means that after taxes the take-home cash adds up to somewhere in the neighborhood of $3,500 per month. If you are single with no children, that amount should cover your basic necessities and allow you to live in a decent part of town. But if you have children, especially school age, that money really doesn't take you far, hence the need for dual household income in America.

When you are an entrepreneur, the host of responsibilities is even more daunting. Time seems to move so fast that keeping up with the bookkeeping becomes the thing most likely to be postponed until tax time or done in haste to get it out of the way, without any analysis or awareness of the actual financial impact the disorganization and lack of planning has on your personal finances and well-being.

My Own Money Struggles

Yes, I have struggled with money issues for most of my life. Just because I am an accountant doesn't mean I've always made the right decisions when it came to money. In fact, I have made terrible decisions that almost led to foreclosure on my house. I was so caught up in my career, my new husband, my toddler, and family issues that I did not have clarity of mind to see that I was getting deeper and deeper in debt.

After moving to the US with a couple of thousand dollars to my name, I ended up working multiple jobs to support myself. I lived modestly in an efficiency apartment (similar to studio apartment) in South Miami. It had a small galley kitchen with the basics. That was more than enough for me since cooking has never really been my thing, and money was too tight to splurge on anything but necessities. Making arepas, a Venezuelan staple made of cornmeal pockets filled with whatever you can find—eggs, ham, chicken, cheese, veggies—was my go-to solution for feeding myself.

The apartment was located on US Highway 1, one of the main roads in Miami, which allowed me to get to my various jobs fairly easily, especially after I saved enough money to purchase an itty bitty Yugo, a cheap, ugly car that got the job done.

The more I learned and developed new skill sets, the higher my earning potential. Eventually, I moved up the corporate ladder and started making a decent salary in my late twenties. I was able to travel abroad to Europe and Mexico. I treated myself to a lifelong dream for a Hawaiian vacation, and at the same time I was helping my parents financially with what I could. This is very much the Latino culture. As you grow up, you are supposed to pitch in financially to support your parents, and I did. All was going well—until it wasn't.

You may remember from the time management chapter that I met Jorge and got pregnant shortly after I began my studies at Nova Southeastern University, a private university in South Florida, to attain the bachelor's degree everyone thought was the key to moving up in the corporate world. I didn't even think pregnancy was possible because I had gone through failed fertility treatments in my previous marriage. But life has a way of making things happen when they should even if we do not understand it.

We both owned our respective homes and decided that the best thing to do was to sell those properties and purchase one family house to raise our daughter and have enough rooms for my parents to live with us. How altruistic of us! We bought a house on a lake. It was a fantastic deal because the house had been rented for over ten years and needed lots of upgrades and care, so the owners agreed to lower the price, and we got our dream house.

We did not anticipate how much the move would cost, or how much more the home insurance would be, or how much labor it would take to get the house in proper living condition, or how much more utilities and household maintenance would cost. We moved into the house, got ourselves some do-it-yourself instruction books from Home Depot, and began the hard work of getting the house fixed. All of it cost money, even doing most of it ourselves. So the credit cards became our solution.

This was in the early 2000s, a few years before the housing crisis of 2008, and house values started going up faster than we could keep up. That combined with more hurricanes caused the cost of living in South Florida to skyrocket. At that point, both our homeowner's insurance and our property taxes were eating up all of our cash, which meant we could not pay the credit card bills or handle any unexpected costs like getting sick or having to replace the broken washing machine.

It seemed that everything cost money—the mortgage, the car payments, the insurance, the school tuition, the utilities, the food, and the list just went on and on. I could not breathe. I would go to bed and cry after getting Gaby to sleep. How had we gotten ourselves into that mess? We both had good wages, yet we could not afford anything. How could we fix it? Where could we get money to get out of that mess?

My resourcefulness kicked in. I started researching ways to reduce our overhead. Selling the house seemed like the most basic solution, but that meant another move and all the costs associated with that. Plus, it takes time to sell a house. So many things to consider, including the fact that my parents were living with us.

At last, the answer came to me: bankruptcy. Ouch! It was the last thing I ever wanted to do after working so hard to move up in the world. A bankruptcy meant a total failure in my mind. I sucked at managing money. I told myself that I would forever have the L scarlet letter on my forehead—you know, L for loser.

After my research, I looked for attorneys who specialized in this type of case. I spoke to a few of them over the phone to find out what the process was, the costs, and what paperwork was needed. I found one who felt like the right fit for us. During the first meeting, my hesitation and fears were obvious, so the attorney told me not to feel bad about it, that even billionaires file for bankruptcy. He walked us through the process and said that it was the smart decision to make, given our family dynamics. (It is not a process for everyone.) We would be able to keep our house, restructure our debt, and eventually sell the house when we were in a better cash position to move. And that is exactly what happened. Three years later, I put the house up for sale, made a good return on the investment, paid off what we owed, and moved to Indian Trail, North Carolina, into a beautiful, brand-new home that needed zero upgrades and had way lower property taxes and homeowner's insurance.

The bankruptcy process taught me many valuable lessons. The most important lesson: if you do not have the cash to pay for something, you do not need it and should not get it. Second most important lesson: find creative ways to make your cash work for you, not the other way around.

I believe I had to go through that hard process in order to truly understand how money works. It was difficult, but it gave me a whole different perspective and allowed me to become even more resourceful in helping my clients and friends. I speak from experience, not from theory. In my house, *cash is king,* a lesson I have passed on to my children.

Secret Struggles

According to statistics published in 2019 by the Small Business Administration (SBA), about 20 percent of business startups fail in the first year. About half succumb to business failure within five years. Now that I have been in business for over ten years, working directly with startups and small business owners, I have firsthand knowledge of the most common reasons small businesses fail: a lack of capital or funding. New business owners often don't understand cash flow or underestimate how much money they will need to get the business started. As a result, they are forced to close before they have a fair chance to succeed, or they struggle unnecessarily and operate in survival mode most of the time.

Although lack of capital is a primary cause for business failure, I want to make sure you realize that the business failing doesn't mean you are a failure. As Fabi Preslar stated in *Fabulous F Words for Business Ownership,* "A business owner who fails is not a failure. You failed simply because there was a better direction, better audience, or better way. Find out what that is and start again." And definitely start by making sure your finances are in order as the first step (2018).

As an accountant with many years of experience, when the situation called for me to start my own business providing bookkeeping services to other small businesses, the first thing I did was run the numbers: best case scenario, worst case scenario, and most likely scenario. I wrote down how much cash I needed to bring into my household bank account to help cover our family's financial obligations. Then I began to list all the expenses this new business would require, fixed and variable. (For the variable I simply wrote an average amount.) Then I added it all up. That gave me the amount of money I needed to bring in as gross revenue per month to break even. It sounds simple because it is! But unfortunately, this is not the way most people going into business think.

As I began to offer my bookkeeping services, I met with many small business owners and solopreneurs. During those meetings, I would try to find out details about their businesses—what kind of systems they were using to track their business transactions, how long they had been in business, what their future goals were—lots of fact-finding questions that allowed me to better understand the business owner and if my services were needed.

An interesting thing started happening. The men I spoke to had no problems discussing their current situations, what they thought they needed in regard to bookkeeping, their goals, and most of all, their desire to hand off this particular tasks to a competent person or company so that they could do more of what made them money. On the other hand, the women I interviewed had a hard time revealing their businesses' financial situations. They spoke in broad terms, or they would just say, "I just don't make enough money yet to be able to afford your services." Mind you, I had not revealed the costs of my services because I was still in the discovery phase, getting to know what the potential client needed and if it would be a good fit. Yet the women had a really hard time talking about money and future growth goals as if they were embarrassed or just unsure of what their numbers actually looked like.

These conversations led me to focus on a new challenge: getting more women aware of their business financials and what it really represented for their own futures. As my business grew and I had a supportive team to handle the day-to-day client demands, I began to use some of my time to educate women who wanted to go into business. I signed up to provide workshops on financial statements, startup budgets, and projections through organizations such as the Women's Business Center of Charlotte and Central Piedmont Community College.

These educational opportunities were important to me in helping women build their businesses. According to a Babson College study, less than 3 percent of venture-capital funded companies have female CEOs (Candida G. Brush 2014). This means that women are starting their own businesses with their own capital, savings, or retirement funds as the primary source of funding their businesses. It seems, at least to me, that women have a hard time revealing their business finances to others (and hence themselves) for fear of being perceived as incompetent or, worse, unqualified to run a business. Nothing could be further from the truth! On the contrary, seeking support from others is actually a great way to evolve from struggling entrepreneur to growth-minded business owner. For growth to happen, we must learn to delegate the functions of our businesses that are not producing our gross revenue.

Having an honest conversation about money and your personal and business situation with a professional who has experience working with businesses and people like you may be the best thing you can do to get unstuck. I often tell my clients that accountants are like attorneys or (if you are religious) priests, where whatever you say and share is kept confidential and should never be divulged. Having an outsider's set of eyes looking into your world can often provide an unbiased opinion and solutions you would not have thought of otherwise.

Developing Your Money-Management Skills (Business or Personal)

Here are some tips to develop your money-management skills:

- **Monitor your cash flow closely.** Don't rely on just the bank balance. Reconcile, or as my daughter calls it "balance," all your accounts regularly. She uses an app on her cell phone to track her budget, then balances that to her checkbook regularly.
- **Make projections frequently**. Set up monthly and annual budgets. Review them against your actual transactions to make sure you are on track. Make adjustments as needed.
- **Identify issues early.** If you lose a client, what does the lost revenue mean to your bottom line and your break-even point? Begin making adjustments to your expenses now instead of waiting until you are knee-deep in bills. If your household income declines, adjust your personal expenses, start clipping coupons, and make sure your family is aware of the financial implications so that everyone acts as a team to save money.
- **Understand basic accounting.** This is so critical to both business and personal financial well-being. Courses are available online to get you started on the basics. Also check out community colleges and nonprofit organizations that offer workshops and counseling to small

business owners and entrepreneurs.

- **Have an emergency backup plan.** You must always have plan B. Examine the what-if scenarios. Having an emergency plan will help you sleep at night.
- **Invoice quickly.** Keeping up with what customers owe you and getting that money as quickly as possible should always be a top priority if you own a business.
- **Use technology wisely and effectively.** This is the twenty-first century. Alexa knows our every move, Siri makes calls for you, and big brother is watching, so why should you not take advantage of technology to simplify your personal life? You can choose from tons of apps to get quick and up-to-the moment information on your financial transactions.
- **Outsource to a trusted provider.** Why should you spend your valuable time doing what others can do better, more efficiently, and at an affordable rate? Spend your time making more deals or enjoying family time.

Here is the thing: you do not have to be a financial genius to manage cash flow. You do, however, have to be steady and regular in that management, so you know exactly where you are financially at any given moment and what you may have to modify if shortfalls occur. There is no shame in admitting you don't know what you don't know. People are out there willing to help and guide you in the areas where you do not feel adequate.

Money is a means to an end. It is a vehicle to take you to the places and experiences you desire. Learn to use it well, and it can support your desired lifestyle..

Your Money Management Stepping-Stones

Break out your journal and write about these questions and thought exercises.

Do you balance your bank and credit cards regularly? If not, why not?

- How much would you need to have in savings to survive if for some reason you had no income for three months (such as illness or job loss)?
- Do you create an annual budget? If so, what do you include? Are you saving money for future purchases? Can you think of five ways you attempted to control your spending?
- When you sit down and send out your bills for the month, are you left feeling good or bad after doing this task? If you feel bad, why?
- Do you know what your personal "break-even" amount is? If not, whose help could you enlist to figure it out?

"I thought to myself, 'That's it. I do not have a choice any longer. I need to pave my own way.'"

13

Trailblazing

While it is true that lots of people become entrepreneurs or intrapreneurs, not all are trailblazers. In order to be a trailblazer, one must have a deep conviction in oneself and a vision, a personal drive that allows you to drive through all the obstacles and roadblocks along the way until you get to your desired destination.

Pave Your Own Way

Have you ever been told your idea is not a good one? Or you do not have the right credentials, experience, accolades, whatever to get job X or to qualify for something you really want? I know I have, many times over. And guess what? Instead of allowing the naysayers to shut down my dreams, I used their no's to motivate me to pave my own way to my dreams.

While working for the software company and after my first daughter was born, I felt I needed a job change to have time to care for my newborn. As a controller, I had way too many responsibilities and stressors that were affecting my family. So I had the brilliant idea to ask my boss, the owner of the company, to allow me to change jobs and become a customer support engineer. It would be a demotion, but I was OK with that as long as it freed up my time to be with my family.

First, he smiled, as he always did with me and my ideas. Then he told me that it was up to the engineering team to decide if I could do the job. So I requested a meeting with the team to present my proposal for my new role in the company. I was told I was not qualified for the job, I had no technical background, I needed to learn X, Y, and Z, and it would take me at least two years to be able to perform at the basic level. Yes, the list of reasons as to why I was not qualified or ready for the job was long. I listened. I took my time to let all of it sink in, and then I began to pave my own way!

I looked at my boss straight in his eyes, ignoring everyone else in the room—not because I was being rude but because I knew that he was the ultimate decision-maker—and asked him directly if he trusted me. He laughed nervously; you see, he was caught off guard by my directness in front of everyone. He said, yes, he trusted me. I then turned to everyone else and said, "All I need is a chance to try it. If I fail, I will move on to another job, to another company." The room went dead silent. After all, the owner had just confirmed that he trusted me.

I started the new position the following month after helping find a replacement for the position I was leaving behind, and as I have done with all of the jobs and challenges I have taken on in my past, I went all in. While getting my baby to sleep at night, I would read database management books. When my house was quiet at night or on the weekends, I would go to the computer and practice SQL queries, run different software tests, read some more, and test my queries over and over again until I felt sure I understood what to do. At the office, I would sit next to the most senior customer engineers to watch and absorb their processes. Nothing better than learning from the pros! Within six months I successfully completed my first project with superlative reviews from the client—and from my coworkers who had been reluctant in letting me have a try at the job. The best affirmation that I had done the right thing by paving my own way was learning that I had become the highest billable support engineer in the company, and clients were requesting to work directly with me. All the while, I had flex time to spend with my family.

Getting Fired

Then there was the time I was working for a local multilocation family-owned business in Charlotte. They hired me as the accounting department manager to help them modernize their processes and clean up the department. They were still using archaic processes to run the day-to-day operations. Some of the accounts payable clerks were killing trees daily by printing every email they received! Dozens of file cabinets took up so much space that it felt suffocating just to walk into the department. And then there was the constant interruption from different people walking in to ask for things and records that could have easily been accessed through technology.

My first couple of weeks on the job, all I did was talk to people within the department and outside of the department to figure out what the gaps and opportunities were before I started firing the people who were not competent, hiring the right people with the correct skill set for the job at hand, upgrading the software applications, and training the staff on new processes. Within one year on the job, I increased the department's productivity and morale. One day while my direct boss was on vacation, the CEO of the company called me to into his office to tell me they no longer needed my services. Yes, I got fired for doing a great job! How about that?

I was in my forties with two daughters, and Jorge's job was undergoing lots of changes and difficulties. After spending a few days crying on my family room sofa and feeling sorry for myself, which is not something I am used to doing (I blame middle age for that reaction), I got up, took a shower, and started job hunting.

I got my first and last job interview with an accounting recruiting firm with offices in Uptown Charlotte. I dressed the part as I usually do, printed my resume on nice paper, and off I went to the interview. I waited a good while past my appointment time before I was greeted by a young, male recruiter who asked me to join him in his office. We proceeded with the usual interview process until he paused after rereading my resume and raised his eyes to meet mine. "To be honest," he said, "I will not be able to place you in the job you are applying for because you do not have any experience working for a Fortune 500 company. Most of our clients are very large corporations." As if accounting skills were not transferable to different industries or business size. People, at the end of the day, you either know your debits from your credits, or you don't!

Needless to say, I was dumbfounded. After eighteen years of experience in accounting and management, this young man was telling me I was underqualified for an accounting job. I stood up, thanked him for his time, left the building, and sat in my car for what seemed like an eternity. What was I supposed to do now? How would I make money, money my family needed to keep a roof over our heads?

I thought to myself, "That's it. I do not have a choice any longer. I need to pave my own way." I went home and spoke to Jorge about what my options were, and he offered to support me in whatever I decided to do next because he knew I was more than capable of making anything work. The next week, I started my own business with a couple thousand dollars that we had in savings, lots of doubts and fears, and a certainty that I was on the right path.

It has been ten years since that interview, and I am so grateful to the young man for telling me I didn't qualify for the job. I am so grateful for that CEO who fired me because I had done such a great job that they no longer needed me. I am so grateful for those engineers who told me I did not have the knowledge needed to do the job. And I am forever grateful to my ex-husband for giving me the vote of confidence I needed to move forward. They were all instrumental in getting me to pave my own way and create a business where we help many small businesses with their accounting needs.

Here's one thing that I've learned that has helped me beyond anything else. We are all on a journey, but the destination is different for everyone. The footsteps you have taken have led you to where you are today. The experiences so far on your journey have helped shape you into the person you are to make you uniquely you. You are not, however, locked into a fixed direction with your next step. Take your talents and your passions and your experiences and think about how you can use those to make the biggest impact on the world. Surround yourself with people who build you up, challenge you, and make you a better person. Listen to your inner voice more instead of to the people around you whose opinions of you don't define who you are or who you want to become. Because on your own journey, you get to pave your own way!

Developing Your Trailblazing Skills

Here are some tips to develop your trailblazing skills:

- **Develop a positive mindset.** This will help you overcome the obstacles you will encounter along the road.
- **Stop prioritizing perfection.** In *Lean In,* Sheryl Sandberg wrote, "Done is better than perfect" (2013). If you put something out that is almost perfect, you can then make small tweaks and adjustments along the way. That's far better than never completing it. For example, this book you are reading—I am sure the next edition will have more insights and details.
- **"Leap before you think you are ready."** Datwon Thomas, a hip-hop journalism pioneer and currently vice president and editor-in-chief of *VIBE* magazine, once said, "You have to pursue your dreams with reckless abandon" (*Becoming Natasha* 2017). In other words, get rid of the thought of failing, of not getting it right. You might not feel ready, but the secret is that you're never going to be ready. There will never be a more perfect time to start your business, or write your book, or get your degree—whatever your dream—than right now. The longer you wait, the more opportunities you miss.
- **Advocate for yourself.** First, you must believe that what you are asking for is what you deserve. Don't ask for less just because it would be easier to get. Customize your request according to who you are asking, and just remember that you become a self-advocate by taking the initiative to

ask directly and specifically for what you need.

- **Start acting as the leader you aspire to be.**
  Thinking and acting like a true leader is the
  only way to become one. In other words,
  walk the talk. Work on your leadership
  skills as you are paving your own way.
- **Play to win.** This simply means focusing on
  what you'd like to achieve rather than what
  you have to lose. If you play to win, give it your
  best shot, and are intentional in what you are
  doing, then you increase your odds to win.
- **Risk failing.** It is OK to fail. It may not feel good,
  but it is without a doubt necessary to learn and to
  succeed. The reality is that if you're never failing,
  you're playing too safe and not giving yourself
  the opportunity to achieve great things in life.

To be a trailblazer, the status quo can't get in your
way. As the famous Dolly Parton once tweeted, "If you
don't like the road you're walking, start paving another
one" (@DollyParton, June 20, 2014). So in the end,
attitude is everything, and with the right mindset, the
sky is the limit.

Who knows better than you what will make you
happy? Believing in yourself as a capable individual
will help determine your long-term success.
Envisioning the life you want is the next step, but you
can't stop there.

At the most basic level, true success comes from
focusing on your own journey, on your own dreams,
and paving your own way toward the life you want. It

does not come from comparing your journey to someone else's and thinking you need to do all the same things in the same order to be successful. Success is not that kind of road. Pave your own way with every stone you lay down. I know the stepping-stones I have laid for my path have led me to the life I dreamed of years ago. I hope yours do too.

Your Trailblazing Stepping-Stones

Break out your journal and write about these questions and thought exercises.

- What path to success do you see yourself paving? Describe it.
- Do you now have the clarity to change the direction of your current path? Where will it lead you? Who will you become?
- What if you took the lessons from your hardships and helped others with similar hardships now pave their way? How would you do it?
- What roadblocks do you think are in your way? How can you remove them?
- What stepping-stones are you laying down on your way to achieving the life you dream of?

"Pave your own way with every stone you lay down. I know the stepping-stones I have laid for my path have led me to the life I dreamed of years ago. I hope yours do too."

Bibliography

Dolly Parton (@DollyParton), Dolly Parton. 2014. "If you don't like the road you're walking, start paving another one." *Twitter.* June 20. https://twitter.com/DollyParton/status/480014214715944960.

Brown, Brené. 2018. *Dare to Lead: Brave Work. Tough Conversations. Whole Hearts.* New York: Random House.

Candida G. Brush, Patricia G. Greene, Lakshmi Balachandra, Amy E. Davis. 2014. *Women Entrepreneurs 2014: Bridging the Gender Gap in Venture Capital.* research study, Wellesley, Massachusetts: Babson College.

Covey, Stephen R. 2004. *The 7 Habits of Highly Effective People: Powerful Lessons in Personal Change.* New York: Free Press.

Harris, Thomas R. 2018. *Get More Done at Work: Advance Your Career. Earn More Money. Impress Your Boss.* Radiant Hope LLC.

Natasha. 2017. *Becoming Natasha.* September 1. Accessed May 27, 2020. https://www.becomingnatasha.com/life/2017/9/1/why-you-need-to-leap-before-youre-ready.

Preslar, Fabi. 2018. *Fabuous F Words of Business Ownership: Redefining Choice Words to Fuel Your Small Business.* Charlotte, North Carolina: SPARK Publications.

Randall, Stacey Brown. 2019. *Generating Business Referrals without Asking: A Simple Five Step Plan to a Referral Explosion.* New York: Morgan James Publishing.

Sandberg, Sheryl. 2013. *Lean In: Women, Work, and the Will to Lead.* New York: Alfred A. Knopf.

Walraven, Erna. 2019. *WIld Leadership: What WIld Animals Teach Us About Leadership.* Wahroonga, Australia: New Holland Publishers.

About the Author

Carolina Aponte is a seasoned professional with more than twenty-five years of experience serving clients both large and small. As the CEO of Caja Holdings, she divides her time between business development, client services, consulting, and analysis. In a span of eight years, Carolina has grown

Caja Holdings' revenue an average of 35 percent year over year. Her business provides outsourced bookkeeping and fractional CFO services to multimillion-dollar companies, law firms, and diverse small businesses, including local accounting firms and nonprofit organizations.

She began her accounting career working on manual ledgers for a Miami law firm. She graduated from Nova Southeastern University with a degree in business management and climbed the corporate ladder at a thriving accounting software company. When she and her family moved to North Carolina, Carolina used her extensive understanding of tax code, accounting, and business management to start a consulting company to provide clients practical and effective internal accounting and tax-reporting solutions.

Carolina serves as the 2020-2021 president of the National Association of Women Business Owners (NAWBO) Charlotte. She holds a Goldman Sachs 10,000 Small Businesses Entrepreneurship certificate and is a Central Piedmont Community College CORE of Business strategic development graduate. Her honors and awards include the 2012 La Noticia Latin American Businesswoman Award, the 2017 NAWBO Charlotte Rising Star Award, the 2019 Mecklenburg Times Phenoms, and the Mecklenburg Times 50 Most Influential Women Class of 2020, and she was a top three finalist in the 2020 NAWBO Charlotte Woman Business Owner of the year award competition.

Pave Your Own Way

13 Skills to Create Your Professional Success

CAROLINA APONTE

Visit **CarolinaAponte.com**
to contact Carolina,
engage with her on social media,
invite her to speak at your event,
and more

Visit **CajaHoldings.com**
to receive valuable tips
on finances and accounting
from the monthly
Caja Holdings newsletter.

9 781943 070961